# Simple Steps to
# Trading
# Discipline

Increasing **Profits** with Habits You Already Have

## TONI HANSEN

FOREWORD BY
LINDA BRADFORD RASCHKE

MARKETPLACE BOOKS®
GLENELG, MARYLAND

D1545987

Publisher: Chris Myers
VP/General Manager: John Boyer
Executive Editor: Jody Costa
Production Editor: Courtney Jenkins
Art Director: Larry Strauss
Layout Design: Jon Jordan
Cover Design: Jennifer Marin

ISBN-10: 1-59280-379-2
ISBN-13: 978-1-59280-379-8

*Printed in the United States of America*

# DEDICATION

A special thank you to my parents and wonderful children for all the support and encouragement they have shown as I have worked on this project and others over the years. I could not have asked for more and will be forever grateful.

# CONTENTS

# CONTENTS

# FOREWORD

I first met Toni many years ago at a conference. She was partners with an associate of mine and every time I ran into them, he seemed to do most of the talking. Thus, I never got to know her very well back in those days. But, as is true in many fields, the people with the keenest insights are often the ones who lie low in the shadows, content to perfect their own approaches, free from outside noise and distractions. There are many excellent traders who have developed their own areas of expertise and their own processes, yet remain relatively unknown—and Toni was originally such a person.

Quite a number of years later, I got to know Toni much better. We had lots in common besides living in Florida. Despite our individual life challenges and being single moms, we both traded every day and spent more hours working then we should, yet still reached out to help others. Toni often traded in the European session since this was the time she could best concentrate on the markets in peace and solitude.

Sometimes the best traders are the ones who talk least about their own personal trading, and I found this to be true in Toni's case. I am astounded that she found the time to write this book. I felt honored when she asked me to take a look at it. Her thoughtful, reflective insights went far beyond a normal self-help book, where too often the word "discipline" is used with abandon. I particularly detest that word because I have yet to consider myself to be "disciplined." I still find myself more than occasionally getting disciplined by the markets.

But Toni's work touches upon one of the important key steps that helped me early on in my trading career. I have also observed the most successful traders and fund managers doing this: writing things down! I once read that if you write something down, it goes to a different part of the brain then if you were to merely just read it. Toni's suggestions on journaling go far beyond keeping a daily diary. It is a complex process designed to lay out a very sophisticated foundation for your individual trading. Tools for developing the basic building blocks cover strategy development, nuances of patterns and structure, (including the "traps" behind many patterns), and go on to analyzing oneself. Are you stronger at trading reversal patterns or continuation patterns? How can you improve the money management functions of certain patterns? What time of day do you trade best?

There is a classic market saying, "If you don't know yourself, the markets are an expensive place to find out." Toni's book covers every corner to help you identify and harness your strengths. She helps you understand your personal Achilles' heel to avoid getting into trouble.

Aside from the fact that this book is an enjoyable read with dozens of tips for traders of all experience levels, each page builds upon the previous to reach a final goal—increasing one's confidence level. This is one of the key ingredients needed for market success. The more detailed your roadmap, the greater the confidence you will have. Sounds so simple, right? Detailed maps help one to gain clarity in the market. Yes, there is some work involved, but I like Toni's phrase, "the cost of not keeping a journal is too high."

 Once upon a time, when I was starting out, I used to write everything down—excerpts from articles and books I read, phrases I heard, patterns I saw, along with detailed record keeping. I never went back and reread anything. And I remember when I moved from  my house in New Jersey, I went through my basement and was overwhelmed by the volumes of notebooks I had accumulated and unfortunately  threw most of them out.  But I think that the initial process of writing things down is what made so much stick in my brain. It gave me a strong foundation to carry me through the last few decades.

Traders are never satisfied with their personal performance. They can always do better, miss fewer trades, manage trades differently, be even more aggressive or conservative when called for, and be better prepared.  Toni's book has inspired me to go back to keeping my notebooks and strive to reach higher still.  Whether you are a new trader just embarking on your journey, or looking for an inspirational read to help you regain some balance in your life, I would be proud to recommend Toni's book. And as for me, old dogs can still learn new tricks.

*Linda Bradford Raschke*

President of LBRGroup, Inc., CTA,
and President of LBR Asset Management

# PART 1

"Whenever a large sample of chaotic elements are taken in hand...an unsuspected and most beautiful form of regularity proves to have been latent all along."

Francis Galton

# TAKING CONTROL OF YOUR FINANCIAL FUTURE

## RAGS-TO-RICHES VERSUS REALITY

As children, we are often weaned on fairy tales. The characters in these stories routinely go from rags to riches with the turn of a few pages. As we grow older, many people still cling to these childhood fantasies. The "adult" versions range from winning the lottery to inheriting a windfall from a long-lost relative. Even though logic tells us that the true path to wealth relies not just on a little bit of luck, but also on a great deal of perseverance and hard work, it is still difficult to not be drawn in by the lure of "easy" money.

There is perhaps no other profession in which the promise of wealth is depicted as an attainable reality to the average individual, no matter what their background, than as a securities trader. There is not a single individual that comes into this field that is not attracted to the promise of financial independence offered by the markets. In the financial arena, the legends of our childhood are revived, and tales abound of men and women beating overwhelming odds to live the lives of which most people can only dream. It has gotten to the point where the formerly homeless, self-made millionaire has even become somewhat of a cliché.

The truth is that the financial markets *really are* one of the few places where fortunes can be made seemingly overnight. It doesn't matter whether an individual grew up in subsidized housing or a penthouse apartment overlooking Central Park. Almost anyone can save up enough to open a small trading account, and, with leverage, turn that small account into a sizable fortune. Although a little bit of luck is necessary—since a trader needs to be "in the right place at the right time" in order to catch some of the best market moves—we also have the ability to greatly influence our own luck when it comes to our trading and investing.

## SUCCESS THROUGH SELF-DISCOVERY

On some days, the markets will move better and offer opportunities that you may recognize more clearly than others. If you have to answer the telephone, use the restroom, or you end up stuck in a meeting when these opportunities develop, then that would be very unlucky indeed. Theoretically, traders could increase their luck by spending every available opportunity following the market. Additionally, they could improve their chances by trading many different types of securities, in order to have a higher probability of locating the marketplace where the greatest momentum moves are taking place on a given day. However, in a world where there is a tradable market virtually 24/7, this is not very practical. For less experienced traders in particular, this may make things even more difficult by hindering their ability to focus and learn the ropes, thus creating even greater confusion.

So for those of you who like to get some sleep every once in awhile and are already overwhelmed by the decision of which direction to turn, you may be wondering just how you can be expected to influence your own luck. The most successful means by far is through the process of self-discovery. Now before you start rolling your eyes at what you may perceive to be some new-age catch phrase, whereby I end up suggesting you head to a mountaintop in Tibet to chant through your nose while standing on one leg with the other up over your head…just hear me out.

- How useful do you think it would be to know the exact times of the day that you will be the most profitable?
- How about being able to know which specific patterns work the best for you at different times of the day?

Take this a step further.

- How would you like to have a very specific checklist of the pros and cons of those specific patterns that will show you what your outcome will be with a very high degree of certainty, and lay out for you a clear plan of action as a trade unfolds?

These questions are merely a few you can answer by using one single tool: **a trading journal**.

# TRACKING YOUR TRADES

A trading journal is a record of your trading activities, experiences, and reflections that is kept on a regular basis. We go through most of our lives as if we're running on autopilot. We don't put a great deal of conscious thought into our actions, and we spend even less time taking steps to change our innate auto-responses to our environment.

This translates into the way that many traders and investors typically approach the markets as well. Instead of controlling their thoughts and emotions, they allow themselves to be controlled by them. Unfortunately, most people's programming is not wired to deal with trying to time the market. When traders fail to override their autopilot, the results are usually mixed, and the growth and development of an individual towards his or her goal of becoming a successful trader or investor is highly stunted at best, or, in the most common scenario, completely curtailed.

Journaling is a powerful method for mapping our auto-response system, allowing us to use that knowledge to implement change. The ultimate goal of keeping a trading journal is to improve our skills, leading to a long and profitable career. Maintaining a journal is as useful to the "newbie" trader as it is the 20-year veteran. The act of putting pen to paper, or fingers to keyboard as the case may be, encourages engagement and reflection. In order to write, we must think. We must put words to our actions, and this fosters objectivity. No matter how attached we may be to an idea, if the results do not support our application of it, we must alter our approach, or toss out our conclusion altogether.

## TONI'S TIPS

### Chapter 1

- The more time you spend following the market, and the more securities you follow, theoretically, the greater your odds will be for locating high probability trades. Nevertheless, this comes with a price. It can prevent you from being able to focus and develop strategies that will allow you to locate, enter, and exit the market's top moves at the most opportune moments.

- Traders and investors typically function on autopilot, yet most have not developed the skills to allow their autopilot to function properly. A manual override is often necessary before reprogramming can commence.

- Implementing and maintaining a trading journal fosters objectivity. It allows you, as a trader or investor, to identify and override faulty, and often emotionally-charged responses to the markets. This will result in the ability to react not only quickly, but also logically and confidently when presented with new trading opportunities.

## A STEP FURTHER

One of the most successful ways a trader can make dramatic progress in their pursuit of a profitable trading or investing career is to implement a trading journal where they can maintain a record documenting their progress, ultimately creating a "guide to action."

What are some of the ways that a trading journal can help you progress as a trader and improve your trading results?

_____

_____

_____

_____

_____

_____

_____

_____

_____

_____

_____

For Toni's answer, go to www.traderslibrary.com/TLEcorner.

# THE ART OF TRADING

There are two parallel skill sets that must be pursued in order to achieve a desirable auto-response program. The first involves developing a focused trading plan or strategy guide, and the second is mastering the art of reading price action in the markets.

## ARTIST TO ANALYST

As a child, I was tutored in the arts, a far different form of artistry than market analysis. My education spanned many genres: from dance to creative writing, to drawing, painting, calligraphy, silk screening, pottery, piano, flute, oboe, guitar, drama, set design, etc. If it was some form of art, I probably tried it. All of these fell under the same heading of "the arts," but it doesn't take a great deal of effort to realize that being a proficient flute player doesn't mean you can draw any better than a third grader. Few realize that when they enter the world of finance, their options are as varied as those of an artist. One of the very first steps that any new trader must take is to narrow down this field and discover the areas of the market for which they have the most natural aptitude.

# NO TWO TRADERS ARE THE SAME

Keeping a trading journal is the single most efficient way of ascertaining where your natural abilities lie. Trading styles do not fall into the "one size fits all" category. In fact, I have yet to meet any two individual traders that are exactly alike. Think about our artist analogy; even if we narrow the field down to impressionist painters, each will have his own unique characteristics that differentiate his work from other impressionist painters. Sure, there are those who specialize in reproducing or copying the works of others, but even they will add touches of individuality to their works.

In trading, there are similar breakdowns in mastery. Some traders will do well with longer-term holds, where they are in a position for several weeks to several months at a time. Others will have difficulty on positions held for more than 15 minutes at a time. Traders also vary in their skill levels based upon the type of markets they trade. Some will excel in futures trading, but will have a more difficult time trading options. Other variations will deal with the type of strategies they employ. Some traders, for instance, may be able to easily see continuation patterns as they form, but will struggle to identify turning points for reversal patterns off market highs or lows.

> Keeping a trading journal is the single most efficient way of ascertaining where your natural abilities lie.

## FINDING YOUR OWN STYLE

Every trader is faced with a great deal of trial and error before they learn what style fits them best. A journal is an excellent medium for recording these trials. When employed correctly, it provides an irrefutable record of past mistakes and accomplishments. At the time, we may not have had enough knowledge or experience to know whether our actions were the correct ones and whether or not they will remain valid over time. A journal will help us recapture those moments so that we can recognize patterns in our auto-response system that either need to be fine-tuned or eradicated.

Given the wide array of possibilities, most traders wonder whether or not the approach they have chosen is the correct one. One very important thing to keep in mind is that no matter which style or genre you begin trading with, the odds are extremely high that as you progress and develop as a trader, you will find yourself drawn to different styles and methodologies than the ones you were originally attracted to. Often what we think is the best style will not live up to our original expectations. Do not let this discourage you! Instead of haphazardly jumping from one end of the spectrum of trading to another—like an artist failing at dance, then turning around and deciding to become a novelist—it's important to examine which aspects of your original style were causing you the greatest difficulty, as well as which parts were your strongest. This will help you take the next logical step.

## EVERY EXPERIENCE COUNTS

In some cases, that next step might appear to be as radical as our hypothetical dancer turned author. Instead of throwing away the knowledge an artist acquires in dance, why not use those past experiences to become an even greater novelist? Perhaps in the dancer's case, she discovers that her body just can't live up to the rigorous hours of intense exertion. Instead of viewing the time she spent dancing as a wash, she can take the emotions she experienced and the lessons she learned while going through that process and use them to help create a dynamic heroine for her novel. If she had kept a journal throughout her stint as a dancer, it would be extremely useful for recapturing those moments of breakthrough and failure to use in the novel, and to develop a character that will really hit a note with her audience. No matter what your focus as a trader evolves into, the knowledge you gain as you work your way through honing your skills in one genre of trading will help you progress more quickly in the next.

# EXPAND AND CONTRACT: THE DEVELOPMENT OF A TRADER

The development of a trader is a process of expansion and contraction. The number of choices to begin with can be overwhelming. First, there is the decision of which type of market to trade, such as futures, stocks, currencies, or options. Then, we must decide what time frame we should focus upon, such as day-trading as opposed to holding positions for several weeks at a time. Additionally, we have to choose the methodologies we wish to employ. This includes the type of analysis we wish to use, the patterns, the indicators, etc. Once a trader has become comfortable with one set of choices, however, the process of expansion once again takes place—where one set of strategies will aid in the development of others. A trader can fairly easily take those strategies and move into other areas of the market using the same skill sets.

## TOUGH DECISIONS –
## THE PATTERN DAY TRADER RULE

Some of the decisions a new trader is faced with may seem easier than others. For instance, if you only have $10,000 to trade with, you cannot make it as an individual day trader in the stock market due to the Pattern Day Trader Rule. This is a National Association of Securities Dealers (NASD) and Securities and Exchange Commission (SEC) rule whereby anyone who is deemed a "pattern day trader" must maintain an equity balance of at least $25,000 in a margin account.

> The Pattern Day Trader Rule is a NASD and SEC regulation stating that any person who buys and sells a security in the same trading day four or more times in any five consecutive business trading days must maintain a balance of at least $25,000 in a margin account.

Traders who fall into this category are those who buy and sell a security in the same trading day four or more times in any five consecutive business trading days. If this is the style of trading that you had your heart set upon, you would have to choose an alternate course, such as trading through a firm, where you add your own funds to the company's capital in order to give you the buying power and avoid the typical restrictions you would have in an individual account.

# WHERE TO BEGIN?

A more common draw for those with under $25,000 in starting capital is the futures or forex (foreign exchange) markets, which allow for smaller account sizes and offer greater margin. This consideration alone should not be taken lightly, however, since traders can more easily manage risk as they learn while trading stocks or less volatile securities. The markets are so diverse these days, however, that there are still many other options. For instance, the CME Group's micro-FX futures contracts offer one alternative to pairs trading in the currency markets, and provide a gateway into that marketplace. You can learn more about what the CME Group has to offer at http://www.cmegroup.com.

The decision regarding which marketplace to enter is one that many traders make based upon hype and popular opinion at the time. In the 1990s, it was the stock market. After the turn of the century, it became E-Mini index futures. Then came the propagation of exchange traded funds (ETFs), and only a year or two later, the focus shifted to forex.

A universal account can be highly beneficial because it allows you to trade a number of securities in one account. If this is not possible with your primary broker, keep a stock account with another brokerage firm to test out strategies in different types of securities using ETFs.

# TRACKING STOCKS AS LEARNING TOOLS

Tracking stocks, in the form of ETFs, are available for everything from oil to currencies, as well as for different sectors that closely follow the price action in the underlying security, index, or sector. For example, if you wish to learn how to trade the Standard & Poor's 500 E-Minis (ES), you can test out your strategies using the Spiders (SPY). The SPY tracks the S&P 500 Index. In the SPY, 500 shares is the equivalent to one E-Mini futures contract. Instead of risking $50 a point trading the E-Mini, you can risk $10 for a comparable move by trading 100 shares of the SPY.

If the PDT (Pattern Day Trader) rule is not an obstacle, ETFs offer a chance to test out different types of markets to find a fit. Let's say that I want to test a certain strategy with a particular security, such as the S&P 500 E-Mini (ES) futures contract. I will use the charts for the ES to establish my entry and exit triggers while executing in the corresponding ETF. In this case, it would be the SPY. This way, I am getting the best feel for how the strategy would translate into the futures position. There will be light variance in the returns generated in the SPY as compared to what a position in the ES would generate due to volatility discrepancies, but it tends to be nominal in the long run. Once you are comfortable trading at least 1500 shares of the SPY, you are likely ready to make the switch to the futures.

# TIME FRAME

Aside from account size, other factors can influence your decision regarding the markets you trade, such as the amount of time you can devote to the markets. For example, if you have a full-time job, you may find it impossible to day trade during the regular trading session, which is from 9:30 am to 4:00 pm EST if you are trading the U.S. markets. This may lead you to securities that can be traded either in the evenings or early morning hours, such as the index futures or forex. Alternately, it may shift your focus towards longer-term strategies such as *swing trading*, which involves holding a position for an average of several days to several weeks. Before you even begin to consider opening a brokerage account, take some time to learn about the numerous options available and what handful of options you feel would likely suit your situation and personality the most. Different brokerage firms specialize in different types of securities, and commissions and rates often vary accordingly.

When I first began trading, I started out as a swing trader in the stock market. In my case, the decision to focus on this time frame and marketplace was not a very difficult one. The stock market was by far the most favored market for online traders at the time and the Pattern Day Trader rule did not yet exist. The main debate was between a fundamental approach versus a technical approach to trading.

> Although the exact amount of time varies depending upon who is providing the definition, swing traders are those who hold a position for anywhere from a full day to a couple of weeks. Three to five days is considered to be average. Swing trades are based upon a trader's attempts to capture a momentum move on a 60-minute to daily time frame using strategies that develop over several days to several weeks.

## FUNDAMENTAL VERSUS TECHNICAL

A fundamental approach involves analyzing the company that you are looking to trade by examining price-to-earnings ratios, growth projections, etc. In the 1990s, this approach was viewed by many as the only legitimate method for investing. Since the stock market meltdown in 2007, which gained momentum in the second half of 2008, this method has come under some scrutiny, but it still remains popular.

Due to my background as an artist and my complete lack of knowledge about the markets, the choice for me was clear. I decided to focus on *technical analysis*, which involves reading the price action of a security in the form of a chart.

> At the beginning of my career, I perused some of the popular texts of the day that attempted to teach fundamental analysis while trying to find my own way. For me, it was very similar to being handed a manuscript written in a language I had never seen before—I just didn't get it. Finding the approach to the markets that makes the most sense to you may take time, but it is well worth it.

Why did I consider the choice to take a technical approach to trading to be the obvious one for myself? Well, from about the time I was a junior in high school, I began to take my experience in the arts and focus on applying it to the field of archaeology. Archaeology is a sub-field of anthropology. Anthropology is essentially the study of how humans interact, grow, and evolve in their habitats. By the time I became interested in the markets, I was already quite familiar with plotting data relating to human nature, so it was a logical step for me to assume that charts depicting price changes in a security were merely the visual representation of human behavior in the markets.

# HUMAN NATURE IN THE MARKETS

Humans are creatures of habit. We react to similar stimuli in similar ways. In the markets, we call this the interplay between greed and fear. In the securities market, this interplay is depicted in the chart of a security and is represented by that security's price action. During the years I studied art, I was able to hone my observational skills to recognize even the most subtle similarities and differences in the world I was recreating on paper or canvas. When I began to delve into technical analysis, I found that I was also able to very quickly ascertain shifts in the price action of a security as represented in a chart, and recall and compare similar developments and their follow-through from the past. This allowed me to project those previous observations onto the future, based on how those factors had influenced the earlier price development.

## REPEAT SITUATIONS

The amount of predictability in the marketplace is still a topic of debate, but most of the people who believe you cannot predict the markets don't have a background in anthropology. They have not spent their lives studying human development and how changes in our environment lead to sets of fairly predictable outcomes. As events progress, the choices become even more narrow, and price shifts in the market reflect these variables with an extreme amount of regularity. Even in markets where many claim that "nothing like this has ever occurred," numerous examples exist of similar price action in the past, although it may take the examination of different securities or time frames to notice them. To date, I have yet to see any type of price development that I have not seen at least a very comparable version of in the past. This includes the 2008 crash, which has taken place on numerous individual stocks on a similar scale, and occurs with even greater regularity on smaller time frames. Such crashes have formed on five-minute charts, particularly in afternoon trades, ever since I first began trading, and I would assume long before that as well.

## WHERE HAVE I SEEN THAT BEFORE?

Traders often have a "eureka moment" in which we say to ourselves, "Hey! I've seen that before!" The difficult part is trying to remember when and where, as well as all of the details that surrounded that previous point in time. Although you may have seen something before that triggers a memory when confronted with a present-day variation, trying to locate useful charts for that previous price development can sometimes be next to impossible. This is especially true if the setup occurred intraday and your charting platform does not allow you to access data far enough in the past to view it again on that same time frame.

A journal, when kept properly, offers traders the opportunity to take immediate action with the ability to go back and examine similar occurrences in the past, without as much frustration as relying on memory alone. The prior entries recorded in a journal can be categorized and can readily serve as a roadmap for guiding your actions on current trades. The more examples you acquire that contain certain sets of parameters, the more detailed your roadmap becomes. In time, the result is a system of rules that define specific actions to take when presented with a specific set of circumstances, or market conditions. This roadmap helps you avoid making costly mistakes in your trading. As you continue reading, I will show you how to construct maps of your own.

A journal, when kept properly, offers traders the opportunity to take immediate action, with the ability to go back and examine similar occurrences in the past, without as much frustration as relying on memory alone.

# A SCIENTIFIC APPROACH

Once I had settled on technical analysis as my primary category for market analysis, with a focus on the stock market, the next decision I had to make was what time frame to focus upon, followed by what strategies I would initially attempt to implement. The first decision was again an easy one. At the time, I was working for the Office of the State Archaeologist during the day, so in order to really participate in the markets, I chose to focus on setups that were forming on a daily time frame. This allowed me to hold my positions for several days to several weeks at a time. In other words, I decided to try my hand at swing trading.

With almost no background in the art of technical analysis, I began to build a trading system. A journal is an integral tool in an anthropologist's professional life, and I found it to be indispensable as a trader as well. Even the most seemingly trivial observation can turn out to be a key to a larger puzzle.

In what had become a habit by that time, I began to employ the basic tenets of the scientific method. According to Merriam-Webster, the scientific method consists of "principles and procedures for the systematic pursuit of knowledge involving the recognition and formulation of a problem, the collection of data through observation and experiment, and the formulation and testing of hypotheses." Hmm…that sounds quite a bit like the definition of a trading journal, does it not?

## IDENTIFYING A PROBLEM

I quickly tossed aside nearly every single book I had been given as a guide to learn how to trade, and instead started very simply. From nearly day one I began to journal. One concept in technical analysis stood out to me. Over and over again, I had been shown examples of how a stock congesting or pulling back for three to five days at a time would be followed by a strong break higher. This breakout strategy seemed to be on everyone's lips. Nevertheless, when I located stocks that were basing on the daily charts or pulling back for three to five days, and bought a breakout from that pullback or base, I found that I could have thrown a dart and been just as lucky. There had to be more to it than merely buying a three to five day pullback. Why would one pullback lead to a sizable upside rally, while another, that looked nearly identical in that immediate daily action, fizzle and flop? Obviously I was missing something, but what?

## GATHERING DATA

Since I did see many examples where this strategy panned out, I began to acquire as many samples of these setups as possible. Not only did I look for setups that worked, but also those that did not. Over time, I developed my own personalized system for analyzing price action in a security. Certain traits, or characteristics, seemed to have greater sway over price action than others. I assigned names to each of these traits, which I felt represented the core building blocks of all price action in the markets. Many years later, these same categories remain unchanged and are the basis for my style of market analysis now taught to traders worldwide. Just think…it is possible only as a result of my journaling efforts over the years!

## FORMING HYPOTHESES

Are all of the building blocks that I use unique? Of course not! In fact, most, in some form or another, have been observed by professional traders for decades. The key is taking these building blocks and learning how to combine them into strategies that fit your own personality. Every trade or setup in a security has pros and cons, and different combinations of these pros and cons affect the outcome of a trade. Just a few of the things they impact are: the odds a trade has for success, the amount of time it takes to achieve a desirable outcome, and the reward the strategy will likely yield as compared to the risk.

Every trader is unique in terms of how aggressive or how risk averse they will be, but having the tools to construct their own personalized strategies is imperative for long-term success. In Chapter 7, I will share with you the basics of the building blocks that I personally use, and throughout this book, I will give you examples of *how* I use them to grow as a trader through the discovery of new patterns, as well as by fine-tuning the methods I already use.

# PLOT PREDICTIONS

The markets are constantly in a state of flux. As they shift, certain strategies come in and out of favor. There are times to press and times to hold back. At first glance, the markets can appear to be extremely chaotic. I think that one of the reasons for this is that most traders look at the market as a series of snapshots. This is what I was doing originally as well. I was looking for those three to five day pullbacks and became quite myopic in my focus. It didn't take long, however, to recognize that the markets are much more fluid in movement.

It is like watching a movie unfold. Anyone who has watched a romantic comedy or a horror flick can make very educated guesses about what comes next. Even if the exact timing or method can't be narrowed down specifically, it is relatively easy to predict how the overall plot will unfold. As each key moment within the movie draws nearer, you can make even more accurate predictions as to exactly when and how they will take place, even though the characters and exact settings vary. As traders, we often begin by focusing on just one scene in the movie, like the first kiss, or the first extra to be killed. These are just a couple of scenes in a larger picture; however, and the more movies we watch, the more experience we gain in predicting the rest of the feature.

Creating a record of your trades over time, such as my example of buying three to five day pullbacks, helps us specialize in those types of setups. It can be similar to fast-forwarding a movie to the first kiss moment and then hitting play as we take notes about the setting, the looks, the moves. At times though, we may see the leading man or woman lean in, as if to deliver the first kiss, only to fail and end up with a peck on the cheek at best—or hair, or even just air, followed by a very awkward moment. The more scenes we watch that end in such a way, the easier it is to see the warning signs coming, whether it's the uncertain, scared, or disgusted look of the opposite partner, or the lights popping on in the house to indicate a parental figure (or child, in my own case) about to swing open the front door. By creating a record of your trades over time, you can start to understand the warning signs in your trade setups that suggest that all might not be hunky-dory, and you can adjust your approach accordingly, to avoid the greatest amount of damage. This is an extremely important part of the developmental process as a trader.

> One of the most important things in your development as a trader is learning to understand the warning signs in your trade setups, and adjusting your approach accordingly to avoid the greatest amount of damage. Creating a record of your trades over time can help you develop this skill.

## PATTERNS EMERGE

Although I began trading by monitoring and dissecting the three to five day corrections in the stock market, many other patterns soon became apparent. As I learned to recognize the traits that would spell disaster for this continuation strategy, a thorough understanding of the development of several high-probability reversal strategies emerged. I also quickly realized the importance of examining multiple time frames when I was trading. Initially, this resulted in better entry and exit timing on my swing trades, but within a relatively short amount of time, I was able to use the strategies I was learning and apply them to setups on the intraday charts as well as the daily ones. Before I knew it, in addition to swing trading, I was also day trading full time.

In time, I started following other markets, from futures to forex. Lo and behold, the exact same methodologies I was applying to the stock market translated very readily to these new types of securities, and I very quickly branched out. Over time, this has resulted in the formulation of strategies that allow me to trade no matter what is going on in my personal or business life. If I have to complete a project and I am up all night working on it, it's not a problem. I will just pull up the futures or forex markets and keep a monitor or two dedicated to those markets. That way, I can keep an eye on them for pattern development while I work on my main project.

As you begin to develop your own strategies, keep an eye out for examples forming on other time frames and in other securities that fall within the same categories. This will give flexibility to your trading style, and will allow you to trade no matter what is happening around you.

This high degree of flexibility came with time. It began with just one pattern on one time frame, which served as the foundation. Every strategy I now use can be traced back to the techniques I first explored and the groundwork I laid through my original journaling efforts.

## TONI'S TIPS

### Chapter 2

- When learning to trade, it's best to always start out slowly and build your knowledge over time. One way to do this is to use exchange traded funds (ETFs) to test out strategies in alternate types of securities, such as futures and forex. That way, you won't need to risk as much per position as you would trading them outright.

- When compiling examples of various setups for a trading journal, seek to acquire as many examples as possible. Include not only examples that led to the results you had anticipated, but also those that failed. This will help you begin to identify both the higher and lower probability variations of a strategy and help you refine your techniques.

- Trading strategies can be built by examining individual components within a setup that can serve as either pros or cons and affect the trade's odds of success, the amount of time it takes to achieve a desirable outcome, and the reward a strategy will likely yield as compared to the amount risked. Such examination will allow you to tailor strategies to suit your own personal risk parameters and personality.

## A STEP FURTHER

There are two parallel skill sets that must be pursued in order to achieve a desired auto-response approach to trading. They are: 1) developing a focused trading plan or strategy guide; and 2) mastering the art of reading price action in the markets.

What are some of the specific steps that can be followed to achieve these goals?

_____

_____

_____

_____

_____

_____

_____

_____

_____

_____

For Toni's answer, go to www.traderslibrary.com/TLEcorner.

# NAVIGATING THE EMOTIONAL HIGHWAY

## NO GUARANTEES

No matter what lured us to the market, whether it was the desire to control our own financial future or to just be able to tell our boss to take a hike, we all envision immediate success. Even though it is virtually impossible to enter this profession without knowing the odds are stacked against you, no one ever truly anticipates total failure. What most aspiring traders and investors fail to realize is that it doesn't matter how smart you are, how many books you've read about the markets, how many seminars or courses you've attended or bought, or even how long you've studied in preparation. None of these things will predict how well you will actually perform on that day when your money is finally on the line. Many of the tools you relied on in the past that might have guaranteed your success in other fields will simply not have the desired outcome when you enter the world of online trading.

# EMOTIONS RUN HIGH

Although books, seminars, preparation, and smarts will help guide you on the right path, in the world of trading, each of these takes a backseat to one highly influential factor: **your emotions**. While it is natural to assume that the development of a trading system requires the mastery of the technical aspects of trading, very few individuals enter this profession with a thorough understanding of the interplay between emotions and logic during this process. Emotions, however, can very easily override the self-control that is essential to rational decision making, and lead your autopilot to run amok.

In trading, you must check your ego at the door. No matter how prepared you think you are, when most traders begin to trade actively, their "fight or flight" programming tends to kick into overdrive. The emotions coursing through your veins are often those that you may not have felt since puberty: confusion, hopelessness, uncertainty, and the feeling that the world is out to get you. You may feel that no one other than your closest friends can understand you, typically because those friends are other fledgling traders. Such relationships can be beneficial, or they can be destructive, just as they were during your adolescent years. In Chapter 10, I will discuss how to cultivate relationships with fellow traders that will dramatically improve your returns. In order to choose our friends wisely, however, we must first know ourselves.

# SELF-REALIZATIONS

I was talking with a fellow trader recently and he made the comment that trading shows you what type of person you really are. You become intimately acquainted with your strengths, as well as your flaws on a level that you had probably never given a great deal of prior thought. The most poignant realizations tend to stem from your insecurities. If you do not deal well with being wrong, then you will have to quickly learn to do so if you wish to thrive in the markets. If you have pressing money-related concerns, these will often come to a head as well. If your relationship with a significant other is rocky, even this will become exacerbated.

As a trader, you will learn more about your best qualities, as well. For instance, you may discover that you are someone who does not give up as easily as you may have thought, or that you can adapt quickly to changing circumstances. You may also learn that you do quite well following a specific set of rules, but struggle if circumstances are vague. Of course, many of us can adhere to certain rules and struggle with others. Identifying which is which can help us build systems that play upon our strengths. Alternately, you may learn that your instincts are usually correct, even without set rules. When this is the case, you may be held back by a lack of confidence in your instincts.

# FINDING CONFIDENCE
# AND MOTIVATION

Like most people, I only gave the topic of how my emotions would impact my success as a trader a passing thought. I certainly did not truly appreciate the extent to which they would guide my decision-making process until I was already quite immersed in the markets. The number of books written about how to deal with the emotional side of trading is paltry compared to those written about how to analyze price action in the markets. I didn't read texts on technical analysis while I was learning to trade, but when I found myself repeatedly making the same mistakes and not trusting my instincts, I turned to books that dealt with the psychology of trading.

I found, however, that applying the techniques propounded in these books was extremely difficult. The advice was typically generic and, although it appealed to me in a common sense sort of fashion, I simply could not get my mind to obey the logic. I continued to act against my own rules, as well as the advice imparted to me in these texts. However, nearly every single one of these texts provided one extremely important influence—a boost of encouragement to keep going, which bolstered my will to succeed. This factor alone was what made many of them worth reading.

They say that if you wish to be successful in life that you should surround yourself with those who already are. You will learn from them and their accomplishments; this will help motivate you to strive to do better and achieve more than you would on your own. Since I did not know many traders when I first began, let alone successful ones, I found a great deal of inspiration from the biographies of people who had triumphed in other walks of life and not merely in the markets.

> For me, the specific information and exercises that were designed to overcome negative emotional responses had very little impact upon my success, although many traders I know have sworn otherwise and found them much easier to apply and stick to than I did.

## LEARNING FROM MISTAKES

While books provided me motivation to continue my career in the markets, it was still necessary to find the means for dealing with emotions that would cause me to hesitate too long when identifying a strong setup, routinely exit winning trades too quickly, and trade much smaller sizes than I should. This is just to name a few of the issues I had to personally overcome. In the end, it was my journal that eventually led me to conquer many of my emotional demons.

Chemist and physicist Marie Curie once said that, "now is the time to understand more so that we may fear less." Making mistakes is part of human nature. We are imperfect creatures who nevertheless seek perfection. We fear the unknown, and this fear drives how we respond to our environment, including our actions in the market. It is this fear that usually causes us to make mistakes.

# FINDING YOUR WAY

As discussed earlier, a trading journal helps us develop a sound trading system. Not only does it show us what works and what doesn't, but in the process, it builds confidence in those observations. The more often we see price action unfolding in a highly repetitive manner, the more certain we become that when future action begins to develop in a similar way, the outcome will be highly predictable.

> There is an infinite number of ways to be successful in the markets, but the driving force behind all of them is having confidence that your system works, and being able to act without hesitation.

## IN TRAFFIC, IN TRADING

How often have you found yourself in traffic trying to navigate unfamiliar territory? Picture yourself rapidly approaching an intersection and you have no idea whether you need to be in the right or left lane to make an upcoming turn, let alone whether you want the most immediate exit or the one after. If you are dealing with city traffic, you may not be able to make it to the far lane in time to catch your exit if you choose incorrectly and if you miss your turn, you may not be able to easily backtrack.

There is a particularly annoying stretch of I-275 coming out of Tampa, Florida, where if you take an exit in one direction, hoping to turn around because you missed your turn earlier, there are no on ramps heading in the opposite direction. In other cases, there are no ramps to return to the highway in the same direction if you exited too early. Since there are only a couple of roads that run north to south for long stretches along the Florida coast, it can be extremely frustrating to try to navigate the territory. In all the times I have found myself having to exit the interstate in that area, not once was I able to quickly pick back up where I needed to—and it took me an average of 45 minutes to get back on track! Just imagine my frustration on each of these occasions where I wove back and forth under the interstate in questionable neighborhoods, attempting to re-enter the highway.

This scenario is not much different from a trader trying to decide what to do when faced with a new position. Instead of on ramps and exit ramps, however, it's a matter of entering or exiting a position in a security. Although I've been forced into an unfamiliar area nearly half a dozen times in the case of my I-275 adventures, should it happen yet again, I am *still* not familiar enough with the area to guarantee that I'll make the best decision the next time around.

## MAPPING IT OUT

I did, however, make a few new observations that would help me improve. If I had drawn out the paths I had taken and written down my observations in the past, it would have been nearly identical to what a trader does when she keeps a journal. I'm averaging about one adventure per year on the aforementioned road, and in each case, I forgot my previous observations until it was too late. The lesson is that good intentions and great ideas will often become just a passing thought if you do not take the time to write them down. If I had been able to pull up the thoughts I'd had during the previous detours, it would have undoubtedly saved me a great deal of hassle and allowed me to make more rational decisions to get back on track.

With GPS and all the toys available to view our current location on the road, and technology telling us which way to go, it may be easy to take for granted a life in which such assistance does not exist. Nevertheless, try to remember a time without these tools, or a time when you attempted to rely on them and they contained mistakes or left out information. Even though my initial excursions up, down, and under I-275 were done without any map, I did attempt to use one the last time around, after recalling my prior difficulty. My lovely two-dimensional assistant failed to note, however, that just because there was a ramp marked on the map, it did not mean that the ramp indicated would allow me to go in the direction I desired!

Likewise, developing a sound trading system from a mechanical standpoint is a much easier task than actually being able to apply it successfully. Nevertheless, the more detailed your own maps are, and the more you navigate a terrain, the more confident you will become that you are taking the correct path. This is true whether you are on a road or in a trade. This confidence will start to override your unintentional responses. You will gain clarity about the markets, about yourself, and the things that affect you and control your actions. Instead of anxiety or hesitation, you will start to respond more quickly and decisively to price action in a security until you reach a point where you no longer question your choices and simply follow through instinctively. The first step is recognizing where you are having difficulty and could use some guidance, just like a location where you have gotten lost in the past.

> The more examples you acquire that contain certain sets of parameters, the more detailed your roadmap becomes. This roadmap helps you avoid making costly mistakes in your trading. As you continue reading, I will show you how to construct maps of your own.

## LEARN FROM GETTING LOST

There are no perfect traders. The main appeal of automated trading systems is that they have the ability to remove emotions from the equation. However, no automated system has the capabilities of an expert analyst. Unfortunately, no matter how long you have been trading, you will continue to make mistakes. Many of your most common mistakes will be easy to pinpoint right away, whereas others may not be noticeable until you start keeping a journal and comparing your trades.

At the heart of a trading journal is the ability to maintain a clear focus upon your destination, both in the course of a specific trade, as well as your long-term goals in the market. By keeping a record of your trials and errors, you can start to develop systems that will assist you in navigating through a trade or market, helping you deal with sticky situations, or avoid them entirely. To this day I continue to make choices that I just want to kick myself for afterwards. Instead of this mental kick coming down the road after a trade has played out, when I can no longer do anything about it, I now tend to recognize it almost immediately. In many cases, this gives me the opportunity to salvage the situation. If I did not have confidence in my system, it would be very difficult to act on the gut feeling that I did something wrong and take immediate steps to correct it.

## TONI'S TIPS

### Chapter 3

- When entering the world of online trading, do not under-estimate the role your emotions will play in your ability to succeed as a trader. Keeping a trading journal can help you build confidence and rise above any negative emotional impulses you may be harboring.

- When being inundated with new data and experiences from one day to the next, you can easily lose sight of the lessons these experiences teach you along the way. Good intentions and great ideas will often become just passing thoughts if you do not take the time to write them down.

- Keeping track of your market and trading observations on a consistent basis is the first step to laying a founda-tion for the development of a trading system that will help you identify and manage opportunities in the market for many years to come. These observations will also help you when your initial strategy does not play out as anticipated by helping you develop the skills to make the most out of an unfortunate situation.

## A STEP FURTHER

A great deal of your success as a trader stems from your ability to control your emotions. Trading has a habit of bringing out both your best traits and your worst flaws. Personal struggles can also become exacerbated once you fully immerse yourself in the markets, so it is imperative to keep these things in mind from the beginning, to consider ways to mitigate conflict, and to draw upon your strengths.

Take a moment to list areas of conflict in your life, personal weaknesses that you may already be aware of, and all of the traits in your personality that you feel will prove beneficial as a trader.

_____

_____

_____

_____

_____

_____

_____

_____

For Toni's answer, go to www.traderslibrary.com/TLEcorner.

# NARROWING YOUR FOCUS TO EXPAND YOUR SKILLS

Nearly every trader I have ever talked to has acknowledged the importance, or at least the perceived importance, of keeping a trading journal. Nevertheless, very few have ever kept one, and still fewer have kept one that has proven useful to their advancement as a trader. As a result, many of those who begin to keep a journal rarely maintain them over the years. A number of things can contribute to this failure. They may not know how to keep a useful journal, they may have tried and failed in the past, or they may not have the knowledge necessary to interpret the data they have collected in their journal.

## FINDING THE RIGHT METHOD

There are a variety of methodologies available for keeping a journal, and this can create some initial confusion for traders. I've tried a number of them myself over the years.

The core types of trading journals involve:

- Spreadsheets
- Notebooks
- Loose-leaf journals
- Blogs
- Online journaling software

Each of these has its staunch proponents, and they are all excellent components of any journaling system. All of these journaling methods have positive qualities that will allow you to learn from them almost immediately and will assist you in making improvements in your trading within just a couple of weeks. However, they are not all interchangeable. They each have their own specific values that will address different skills, although some of these qualities will overlap from one style to the next. It is neither necessary, nor advisable, to attempt to maintain each of these types of journals simultaneously. Some traders will find that one form suits them very well, while another may be too cumbersome to maintain for extended periods of time.

As you continue reading and learning about the different types of journaling, you will undoubtedly find some methods more suitable for your particular career than others. You will also see how each type has lessons you can learn from more easily than others. As you work your way through trades and study your mindset as a trader, you will likely focus upon one style of journaling more closely than another until you decide to move into another area of interest for improving your skills.

As you develop your journal, it will help you identify your strengths and weaknesses so that you can exploit and overcome them, respectively. After a couple of weeks, read over the data you have collected, identifying one or two points to focus on. There are always going to be things you need to improve, so don't worry about trying to identify all of them at once. Although it's beneficial to learn as much about your trading style as possible, it's extremely important to not pursue all angles simultaneously.

You may be thinking: If I consider all of these to be useful components for a journal system, then such a system will quickly become unmanageable. But, this will only be the case if you let it be.

A great way to think of developing your trading journal is just as you would the development of any system. Start small with tasks that will begin to show immediate results. You may wish to keep track of some additional data along the way to help you with more in-depth analysis later, but don't try to tackle everything at once.

As you read through each of the methods for maintaining a journal, start by selecting only one or two. They should be in a format that fits easily into your trading day and won't take up more than about an hour or so of your time per day during your non-trading hours. If you feel overwhelmed by the exponential amount of data you are trying to collect and analyze, then the chances are high that you will not be able to maintain a journal of that caliber for very long. The process of journaling is meant to aid you with system development over time, and help guide you in your choices as a trader. If you are trying to keep a journal that you cannot sustain, then there is very little point in attempting it in the first place.

Numerous studies have been published that emphasize the fact that multi-tasking diminishes our ability to think clearly and rationally. It's easy to believe that the more information we have, the better our decision-making abilities. This is a false premise. In fact, the amount of additional information may actually distort your decisions by pulling your focus away from the core problem you are trying to solve. One risk is that it can inundate you with a lot of irrelevant data for the task at hand. It will also likely bring to light other issues and concerns that you need to eventually address. This would make it very easy to become distracted, as well as overwhelmed. Keep it simple to begin with and work on improving one skill at a time.

# TONI'S TIPS

## Chapter 4

- The most popular forms of journaling include spreadsheets, notebooks, loose-leaf binders, blogs, and online journals programs. Each of the different styles of journaling will offer unique insights into your trading that may not be readily apparent when using another style.

- Attempting to implement and maintain several styles of journaling at once, however, is neither necessary, nor practical. A practical trading journal is one that you can easily maintain over time without becoming overwhelmed by the amount of data you are collecting and analyzing.

- Trading journals will bring to light many areas in your strategies, and the application of your strategies, that will need improvement. Stay focused and tackle one obstacle at a time.

For more trading tips, go to www.traderslibrary.com/TLEcorner.

# PART 2

"Those that do not learn from their ways are condemned to repeat them."

Anonymous

# 5

# TRADE LOGS

A simple way to begin recording your trades is to keep a log of your trading activity. Many traders do so in the form of a spreadsheet. Most traders use these spreadsheets to track basic accounting data, as well as trade data such as entry points, exit points, gains, and losses. When I ask a trader whether or not they keep a trading journal, when they say, "Yes," they are usually not keeping a journal per se, but rather a spreadsheet of their trading activities.

A trading log is purely a statement of facts. Figure 5.1 depicts what a typical trade log looks like. It can be helpful for tracking your progress day by day from the perspective of your fiscal performance. This data alone, however, offers very little insight into the skills and weaknesses of a trader. In order to qualify as a journal, there must be a component that allows for *analysis* and *reflection* that can lead to a system for improving your results. Although it does not serve as a journal in and of itself, a trading log can still be a very important component of any journal when applied correctly.

# CHARTING YOUR PROGRESS

Due to the fact that a trading log is a collection of measurable or quantifiable data, it offers the opportunity to track the data collected in the form of a chart to facilitate data analysis. The most basic data that many traders collect or monitor from day to day is their account balance. It is a simple process to take this information and track it in the form of a line graph, like the one in Figure 5.2. Charting your performance in this manner is one of those things that can serve as a great asset, or a great hindrance to your success.

What many traders don't realize is that their own performance is just like that of any company or mutual fund. Patterns develop and play out with accuracy comparable to those of any security. Once you learn how to read price action in a security well, you can take that knowledge and use it to help you recognize when you have an edge that you can press in the markets, or when things are starting to shift and a potentially more difficult time is coming up that may have a negative effect on your performance.

Tracking your account equity has the potential to negatively impact how you trade, so you will need to pay close attention to this possibility and change your approach if you believe this may be true. Try it out for awhile, and if you feel that it is something you obsess about, then put it aside for awhile, or move up to a larger time frame and track only your weekly or monthly performance as opposed to your day-to-day results.

The main risk is that when things become more difficult in the markets, you might begin to see patterns forming (on the chart de-

# FIGURE 5.1: HYPOTHETICAL TRADE LOG

| Date | Security | Direction | Entry Time (ET) | Entry Price | Exit Time (ET) | Exit Price | Points | Size | Result | Commissions |
|---|---|---|---|---|---|---|---|---|---|---|
| 4/6/2009 | ES | long | 9.54 | 826.75 | 10:11 | 829.75 | 3 | 4 contracts | $600.00 | ($19.00) |
| 4/6/2009 | ES | long | 10.24 | 827.25 | 10:27 | 825.75 | -2 | 4 contracts | ($400.00) | ($19.00) |
| 4/6/2009 | ES | long | 10:39 | | | 825.75 | 0.5 | 3 contracts | $75.00 | ($14.25) |
| 4/6/2009 | ES | short | 11:00 | | | 822.75 | 2 | 4 contracts | $400.00 | ($19.00) |
| | | | | | | | | | $675.00 | ($71.25) |
| | | | | | | | | Commissions: | ($71.25) | |
| | | | | | | | | Total: | **603.75** | |

For a closer look at this chart, go to www.traderslibrary.com/TLEcorner.

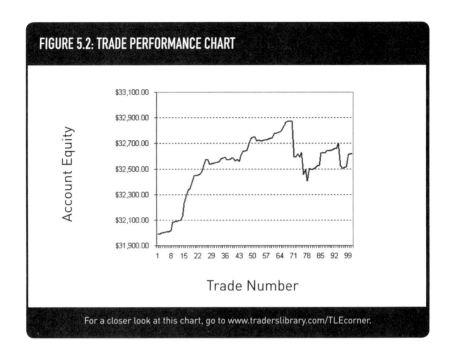

**FIGURE 5.2: TRADE PERFORMANCE CHART**

For a closer look at this chart, go to www.traderslibrary.com/TLEcorner.

picting your account changes) that indicate the higher odds of an upcoming correction off highs. Instead of your account remaining virtually flat with a correction taking place through a trading range, the realization that a correction has a higher chance of forming can trigger that correction prematurely, or lead to a deeper correction than you would have experienced otherwise—all as a result of emotions coming into play and negatively affecting how you trade.

On the other hand, the knowledge that your results are starting to show greater corrective potential can help you reduce risk at these levels. It can also allow you to correct over time, even if there is a period of congestion during which the markets play out a phase that is less favorable to your trading or investing style. Instead of getting hit with a larger drawdown by trading as usual, this can help you can step back and achieve a more desirable outcome by lowering your risk exposure until you begin to see more favorable action develop.

# TRADE TIMING AND TUNNEL VISION

Over the years, I've worked with thousands of traders. One of the most common situations that day traders experience is that if they stay glued to their desks and their screens from the opening bell into the closing bell, then they will often have their best performance in the mornings. This can occur whether they are playing the opening momentum, or if they are waiting until after the initial action has taken place and are trading continuation or reversal strategies somewhat later in the morning.

After approximately 11:00-11:30 EST, many traders that participated in the markets throughout the morning will begin to struggle. Tracking your performance according to the time of the day can reveal this very quickly and allow you to develop strategies for dealing with it if this proves to be the case. For some, the best option is to trade for the first several hours of the day and then do one of two things: 1) take a break for an hour or two over lunch and then come back in the afternoon, or 2) focus on trading only in the mornings and then find something else to do (other than trading) during the remainder of the session.

A primary cause for this situation is that when you don't take the time to step away from trading intraday, it can become easy to lose track of the bigger picture. As you become settled into your routine, your reaction time can slow as your body and mind enter a conscious state of rest. This leads to a third alternative solution to our common dilemma: taking a few 5-15 minute breaks throughout the day can help combat this natural progression in our physiology. Some traders, however, find it difficult to pull themselves away for even this long.

I must confess that physically removing myself from my desk during the day can be difficult for me as well. It's always in the back of my head that if I step away, then I might miss a great opportunity. The one thing that convinced me to do so anyway was my own observation that after short breaks, I returned with a fresh point of view. When I sat back down to trade, setups seemingly jumped out at me and caught my attention almost immediately and with very little effort. I was able to make quick decisions without over-analyzing them, and I was less emotionally attached. With the help of journaling, I found that these breaks served the same purpose for me that taking a long lunch break or trading only half the day served for others.

Everyone has different times that work best for them and these can shift over time, just as they do for me. Keeping track of your performance during your different trading hours can help steer you in the right direction to maximize those periods during the day where your efforts will produce the greatest rewards.

Not everyone will find the morning to be the easiest time to trade. For others, it might be the afternoon or evening that suits their personality and lifestyle. When I am working on a project, I will often trade the early morning hours here in the United States when the markets are active overseas. The house is quiet and there are relatively few distractions. Since most of the people I know are sleeping, it is easy to keep a few charts open while I take care of other business.

## USING SPREADSHEETS TO TIME TRADES

Tracking your monetary performance is an obvious use of a trading log, but this type of tool also has the potential to offer a number of insights on the basic style of trading that you may favor. In order to achieve this goal, though, the trading log must go beyond merely tracking a security's symbol, entry price, exit price, and the resulting gain or loss.

Including both the entry and exit times is one way to make a trading log more useful. This data can be used to identify the times of the day when you are the most successful. This makes it of particular interest to day traders. They enter and exit their positions within the same trading session, and many who fall into this category will often experience their peak performance during narrow spans of time intraday.

The "sweet spot" for some day traders occurs right after the opening bell. This is a particularly lucrative time for those traders who focus on gaps and opening momentum plays. Gaps occur when a security ends one session at one price, and then opens at another price the next day. Strategies based upon gaps are very popular in a number of securities, such as in the stocks and futures markets, and it is common to see the strongest moves of the day take place in these securities soon after the session begins. Figure 5.3 shows examples of extreme gaps in Apollo Group, Inc. (APOL). Extreme gaps such as these, however, can have a more difficult time following through intraday past the first 45 minutes of the session. I typically focus on those that are approximately half the size of the ones depicted here.

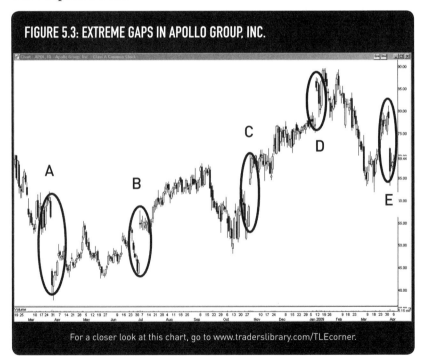

FIGURE 5.3: EXTREME GAPS IN APOLLO GROUP, INC.

For a closer look at this chart, go to www.traderslibrary.com/TLEcorner.

Although the opening momentum may offer some traders the best opportunities for the day, for others, this time period can cause a lot of anxiety, and attempts to participate can lead to more numerous mistakes than during the remainder of the session. If you observe this fact in your trading log, you can avoid the opening action in favor of less volatile price development and setups that develop over longer periods of time. This "lead-in time" can help you plan your attack more thoroughly and with greater confidence.

## ENTRIES & EXITS

In addition to intraday "sweet spots," a trading log that tracks entry and exit times can also show which days of the week and times of the year are the most profitable for you. It will take longer for this data to prove itself, but it will help you prepare for the future so that you can adjust your trading to accommodate the odds. When examining this data, consider adding notes such as which days are shortened trading days, major news days, days you are sick, etc. This is where other forms of journaling will come into play.

## VISUALIZING YOUR DATA

There are a number of ways to take this data from a Microsoft Excel spreadsheet and use charts to help you analyze it from a more visual perspective. One way to examine your entry and exit timing is to create a series of pie charts. For example, you can analyze your entry data by creating two different charts. One can depict the data for your winning trades, while the other can depict your losing trades. Divide the day into increments of time and track the percentage of trades that you enter during those time periods.

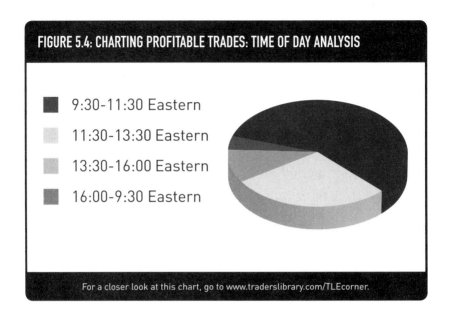

FIGURE 5.4: CHARTING PROFITABLE TRADES: TIME OF DAY ANALYSIS

- 9:30-11:30 Eastern
- 11:30-13:30 Eastern
- 13:30-16:00 Eastern
- 16:00-9:30 Eastern

For a closer look at this chart, go to www.traderslibrary.com/TLEcorner.

This is shown in Figure 5.4. Now, take this a step further. When you have identified specific increments of time that show the most intriguing data, you can divide these into smaller increments. For example, divide the first two hours of the day into 15-minute increments to more specifically identify the times of the day during which you are entering your best positions.

Another way to track your entry data is to include both your winning and losing positions in one chart. These charts would look similar to Figure 5.4. Instead of showing the percentage of winning trades taking place within each segment of the pie, however, each segment of the pie would represent how many trades took place during those periods of time. Each segment would then be partitioned according to winning positions and losing positions. Ideally, this would be done by using two different colors on top of different textured backgrounds. Using the same analysis strategy, a chart created to depict your exit timing would look essentially like the one in Figure 5.4.

Keep in mind that not all trades end up as strong winners or losers. Sometimes the results are closer to break even. To examine this particular topic, you could create a third chart showing the entry times for those that were approximately break even, give or take a certain dollar, tick, pip, or percentage amount. When examining the number of trades taken at different times, you could also divide this into three segments instead of two (profit or loss) to take into account trades with negligible gains/losses. This should be considered throughout your journal analysis and used in conjunction with other results, such as your average holding period.

The nice thing about including charts in your spreadsheets is that once you have the formula created for the chart, it doesn't require much maintenance other than data entry. Granted, if you are not very computer-literate, or at least Microsoft Excel-literate, it can take a full day learning how to create and then make all of the charts you wish to associate with your trading log. Nevertheless, spending a day learning how to create such graphs is typically well worth it in the long run.

> Using charts to track your trading can help you to easily visualize your performance, revealing a number of insights on the basic style of trading that you may favor.

## TIME FRAME ANALYSIS WITH SPREADSHEETS

As I stated above, a column that tracks the average time that you spend in a position or trade is another field that can be added to a spreadsheet to make it more informative as a systems development tool. Namely, it will allow you to identify the average holding period for your best and worst performing setups, and it can be used to further advance the knowledge you ascertained by examining your entry and exit timing.

There are several ways to interpret such data. On the one hand, tracking your average holding period can help steer you into the best time frames that complement your personality and lifestyle. If your performance is the strongest on trades that you hold for an average of 15-60 minutes, as in Figure 5.5, and worse on positions that you are holding for multiple days, it may be reasonable to conclude that you should stick to day trading. Although you may wish

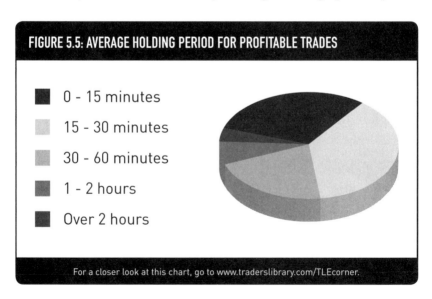

**FIGURE 5.5: AVERAGE HOLDING PERIOD FOR PROFITABLE TRADES**

- 0 - 15 minutes
- 15 - 30 minutes
- 30 - 60 minutes
- 1 - 2 hours
- Over 2 hours

For a closer look at this chart, go to www.traderslibrary.com/TLEcorner.

to focus on longer-term setups, it might take longer to develop and master strategies on those time frames. In the meantime, you can supplement that learning curve through intraday activity.

A pie chart is also very useful for analyzing this data. You can display the percentage of trades held under 15 minutes, held from 15-30 minutes, 30-60 minutes, 60 minutes to 2 hours, 2-4 hours, 4-6 hours, 1 day, 2 days, 3-5 days, 1-2 weeks, etc. Just glance through your trades to determine how to divide the time. If most of your trades are held for less than 2 hours, then you can simplify things by just creating a final category that is 2+ hours.

Each of these slices of pie can then be divided into the percentage that were profitable and the percentage that failed. Once again, you will have many positions that were closed without a strong gain or loss, so you may wish to consider dividing each pie segment into three portions to take this into account as well. The easiest way is to take a chart like the one in Figure 5.5 without the use of a black slice of pie, and divide each portion into two or three colors: green for the winning positions, blue for the positions with miniscule gains or losses, and red for the losers.

## MAKING JUDGMENTS

Don't be too quick to judge. Even though this data may suggest that you show the greatest potential on intraday trades, there can be another interpretation to explain why the greatest percentage of your winning trades takes place intraday. By adding several additional columns, you can gain a better handle on the accuracy of such an observation. Each of these columns deals with time frame analysis.

A column that identifies the primary time frame upon which your setup occurred is one way you can enhance your observational skills. For example, this could be a daily chart for a breakout or a five-minute chart for a bull flag intraday. If the number of trades occurring on a smaller time frame is greater than those occurring on a larger time frame, then an observation that you perform better on smaller time frames based upon the average holding period of your best and worst performers may be inaccurate. That difference could merely be a reflection of the greater number of trades taken on the smaller time frames.

This type of column can be somewhat subjective because a setup may be apparent on multiple time frames. That's okay. It doesn't have to be an exact science. One of the things I like to consider is: which chart caught my attention when I first pulled up the security? Was it the five-minute chart that grabbed my eye, or was it the daily chart? Even though I prefer that setups have confirmation on multiple time frames, these will just add to my original bias. It is that original bias, however, that is tracked in this particular column.

Another column can be added that backs up this original urge to place a trade. Include a simple "yes" or "no" regarding whether the setup took place in the direction of the larger time frame bias or not. For example, if a buy setup forms intraday, but it also has a lot of room on the daily chart for more upside, then this is going to serve as a major pro in favor of the setup and can increase its odds of success. Knowing which setups had this bias and which did not can help you understand why a strategy worked in one instance, or why it failed in another.

When I am day trading, I will often find a strategy on a five-minute time frame that lures me into exploring it more thoroughly for its potential. I will then drop down and use another setup on a smaller time frame to time a better entry on the setup I located on the larger time frame. One of my own observations over time was that when I do this, I typically have much greater returns and smaller stops. Stops are the price levels that a setup should hold if your original hypothesis is correct. If my stop price hits, it tells me that I most likely made a mistake, and I will close the position. Using smaller time frames to look for lower risk entries does have a drawback. If I fail to take a setup because I cannot locate a more ideal entry on the smaller time frame, then I may miss out on a great opportunity. A column in your trading log that identifies whether you used a smaller time frame for managing a position can help you discover if the attempt to do so is hindering you or

You could also add a column that gives a yes-or-no answer to whether or not you used a smaller time frame for timing your entry and exits than the time frame displaying the price action that originally caught your attention. These results can also be displayed in a pie chart, or merely as percentage results at the bottom of the column.

helping you. They can also help you identify the conditions within the security's price development that make the most difference. Tools for analyzing these conditions will be explored in Chapter 7.

Although it might be easy to add a column to your trade log that identifies the time frame you used to locate a setup, it can take longer to develop your skills to read the larger time frame bias. You can begin by noting whether a trade takes place in the direction of the trend that is intact on the time frame in question, or whether the trade goes against it.

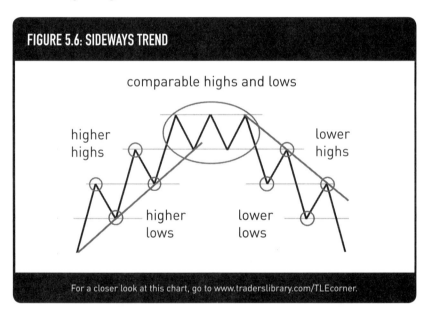

**FIGURE 5.6: SIDEWAYS TREND**

comparable highs and lows

higher highs

lower highs

higher lows

lower lows

For a closer look at this chart, go to www.traderslibrary.com/TLEcorner.

A buy setup that takes place as part of a series of higher highs and higher lows on a chart of a security occurs in the direction of the trend. In this case, the trend is an uptrend. If there are lower highs and lower lows when a buy setup occurs, meaning that a down-trend is in place, then a buy setup would go against the trend. If the highs and lows are comparable (see Figure 5.6), then you will have to step back to the next larger time frame to determine whether it is with or against the larger trend. This can help you identify whether you are stronger at continuation patterns or reversal set-ups. At the very least, it can help you avoid using certain setups when they go against your trend bias.

## HOLDING TIME

Let's backtrack for a moment and once again examine the average holding time on your positions. While the above analyses deal with your observational skills as they apply to the markets, measuring the length you typically hold a position can also reflect your strengths and weaknesses from an emotional standpoint.

If you discover that you experience greater losses when you hold for the shortest amount of time, this can indicate a lack of confidence in your positions, as opposed to a problem with short-term trading. This is often the case when the trades themselves work out over a greater period of time, but something caused you to bail on the positions more quickly than you should have, and prevented you from achieving your objective.

To make better use of this data, add another field to your trading log that includes your original target on the position and whether or not it hit. If you discover that your targets are hitting more often than not, and yet you are still exiting positions very quickly with a loss or mediocre gain, this knowledge can help you implement safety measures that will allow you to more easily hold a position into a target zone instead of panicking with an early exit.

## ONE CANCELS ALL

Knowing that your targets would most likely hit can be enough to help mend your ways. If it is not, however, another way to do so is to adjust the types of orders you are using. This particular issue is one that has plagued me over the years. When I find myself slipping up, it is usually because I am not holding onto my trades into their target zones. The best way that I have found to overcome my bad habit of bailing too early is to step away. To do this safely, I will place what is called a "one-cancels-all" order. This is a type of bracket order in which you enter your target order and a stop at the same time. A stop is the maximum amount you are willing to risk before you admit that your original assessment was incorrect.

In a "one-cancels-all" order, when one of the orders is triggered, all other orders that are associated with it will immediately be cancelled. If my target hits, my stop order is cancelled and vice versa. To avoid overriding these orders manually, I will find something to distract myself for awhile while the setup has time to begin to play out. I may scan for additional trades, answer some email, play solitaire, etc. By physically pulling my attention away from the trade and letting the odds take care of themselves, I can profit from the knowledge gleaned from my trading journal that my targets will hold true more often than not.

# WHAT TO TRADE?

Another useful aspect of a trade log is that it tracks the securities you are trading. By doing so, it can help you identify which securities are the most lucrative for you to trade or invest in, and which you should avoid. This can be particularly beneficial when you are first starting out and trying to find the best path to follow. Some traders can identify setups or execute positions in certain securities more easily than they can in others, and it's often a matter of trial and error to ascertain which is which.

By tracking the performance of trades in different securities, it can help you narrow the field down to one category, such as futures or stocks. This can then be taken a step further. The field can be narrowed down to a specific futures contract or basket of stocks that you have the best track record with, allowing you to pay greater attention to these setups as the core focus of your activities.

## STOCKS

Traders that focus on stocks can use a trade log to help them narrow down the possibilities according to price and volume. Most stock traders have a price range that feels comfortable to them. Some prefer stocks trading over $50 a share, while others have a knack for so-called "penny stocks." This term is most commonly associated with stocks that are considered highly speculative because they tend to have low market capitalization and trade under $5 a share. Some traders may also do extremely well trading the more volatile securities such as Google (GOOG) in Figure 5.7, which are very liquid, but experience large and extreme prices changes intraday. Others may find such volatility nearly impossible for them to manage easily. At the beginning of 2009, for example, GOOG typically experienced a price range of over $1.00 on an average five-minute bar.

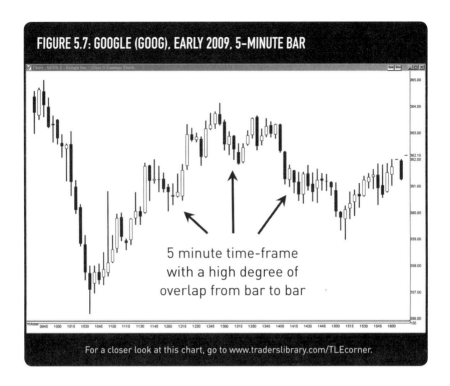

FIGURE 5.7: GOOGLE (GOOG), EARLY 2009, 5-MINUTE BAR

5 minute time-frame
with a high degree of
overlap from bar to bar

For a closer look at this chart, go to www.traderslibrary.com/TLEcorner.

I prefer to stick to companies that are well-capitalized and trade between $10 and $150 a share. One way to quickly judge more volatile price action is to look at a chart of the security in question.

For example, if the price range for one five-minute time frame in a stock I will refer to as XYZ moves from a low of $100.00 to a high of $100.50, and the next five minutes trade in a range with lows of $100.10 and highs of $100.60, then there is a high degree of overlap from one bar to the next. Let's compare this to a stock I will refer to as ABC, which has a five-minute range of $100.00 to $100.50 and is followed by a second five-minute increment where the lows are $100.45 and the highs are $100.95. One that routinely trades like XYZ, particularly when it is in either an established up-

trend or downtrend, will be a higher risk than one that trades like
ABC when it is actively trending higher or lower.

## FINDING YOUR OWN NICHE

Developing a focus on a particular security, such as an E-Mini futures contract or a specific stock, is a great way to advance your
skills as an analyst and trader. It is important, however, to realize
that the types of securities that are the most favorable at present
can easily fall out of favor and fail to offer similar opportunities in
the future. How they perform can shift dramatically in a very short
period of time.

Niche companies such as Crocs, Inc. (CROX) in Figure 5.8 are no-
torious for short-lived stints in the limelight. CROX broke free of a

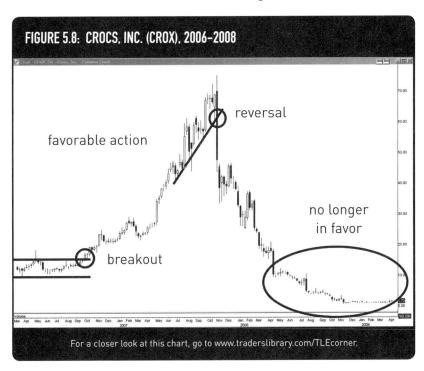

FIGURE 5.8: CROCS, INC. (CROX), 2006–2008

For a closer look at this chart, go to www.traderslibrary.com/TLEcorner.

trading range between $10 and $15 a share in late 2006. From that point throughout 2007, it offered a plethora of opportunities for everyone from intraday scalpers to position traders. The uptrend exhausted itself into the end of October 2007, and the aftermath was quite violent. It continued to be widely followed by day traders well into 2008, but declining volume and falling prices led traders to other venues, and CROX fell out of favor with the mainstream crowd by the middle of 2008.

Do not become so attached to a security that when it falls out of favor, you fail to acknowledge that fact. Securities such as CROX will generate mild attention from time to time, but the higher risk associated with trading them will keep them on the fringe unless a fundamental development within the company launches them back into the mainstream.

The opposite can also happen. Stocks or other securities that were not widely followed can gain interest over time and begin to perform in a manner more favorable to trading than they were in the past. This is common when companies expand, make new discoveries, successfully launch new product lines, etc. A dramatic increase in volume is one of the first indications that something is afoot. This is often accompanied by a price breakout from the range in which the stock had previously been trading, similar to the breakout in CROX in the second half of 2006.

# DEVELOPING GUIDELINES FOR TRADING STRATEGIES

Be aware that markets change over time, and strategies for trading in certain market conditions will be affected. By assigning a name to each of your trading setups that share a significant number of similarities in how they develop, you can make further use of a trade log. In order to do this well, you must first develop guidelines for your trading strategies. A lot of traders will take a position simply because they feel instinctively driven to do so. These instincts are sometimes correct, while at other times they are not. If you can develop a set of guidelines for the trades you take, then you can begin to classify them.

## NAMING YOUR SETUPS

When you assign names to your setups, it is best to start with a more general label. Over time you can narrow them down, but this will help keep your data manageable in the beginning. This will also help you locate your strongest types of strategies. Once you have made this determination, then you can start to focus on more of the details and subdivide your trades accordingly.

Some of the mainstream names for different strategies include breakouts, head and shoulders patterns, triangles, bull flags, and bear flags. The list is endless when you consider the complex variations and tools that traders apply when developing their own strategies. If you stick to using names that bring to mind a visual representation of what you are trading, then it can make your analysis a little easier.

As you start to tweak different variations within a category, you will need to add further classifications. A typical example is a triangle setup. When technical analysts refer to a triangle, they are describing a period of time in which the price range of a security is narrowing. This creates a formation that looks like a triangle. This classification can be further divided into subcategories such as ascending, descending, and symmetrical triangles.

As you gain experience trading triangles, you can narrow these even further. Symmetrical triangles can be both reversal and continuation patterns. They can even create traps where they trigger a false setup in one direction, and then a stronger reversal in the opposite direction. The five building blocks that I use to create the various patterns or strategies that I trade, which I will talk about in Chapter 7, offer a solid methodology for identifying traits within a setup. You will learn to recognize key differences to help you create narrower categories for your strategies.

## ADJUSTING YOUR SETUPS

As the market or individual securities develop over time, the best strategies to play on a given day may also shift. Sometimes a particular setup will be plentiful, while at other times you may have difficulty locating it without additional cons attached. These cons can have two effects. They can increase your risk of failure and lower the percent of trades that hit their typical target levels. Additionally, they can make it necessary to aim for lower overall targets.

If the securities you trade don't offer the same types of setups or returns they did when you first began, then it may be time to regroup and devote more time to studying your trades, as well as the market. This can result in improvements in your strategy to deal with the changes, or it can force you to explore other vehicles to expand your repertoire of securities and/or strategies.

## TONI'S TIPS

### Chapter 5

- Charting changes in your account equity will reveal patterns similar to those that take place in individual securities. Once you learn how to read price action in securities, you can take that knowledge and use it to help you recognize when you have an edge that you can press in the markets, or when it would be best to back off and reassess your current approach.

- A common dilemma for many day traders is that they will experience their best performance within the same span of time intraday from one day to the next. A trade log can help you identify when your peak performance typically occurs during a trading day.

- When you spend prolonged periods of time at one task, you can start to lose your edge. Your body will begin to enter a state of rest. Taking breaks throughout the day will allow you to refresh and refocus. Often, new setups will seem to leap to your attention upon your return, particularly once you learn to time your breaks according to the development of the market's trend and your intraday performance peaks and valleys.

- A pie chart can help you visualize how long you hold your most successful and least successful positions, helping you to determine an ideal time frame on which to focus. This can also point towards a lack of confidence and the fact that you might be letting your emotions rule your trading as opposed to logic. This will be apparent if you are scalping most of your winners, while holding your losers for substantially longer periods of time.

- Once you locate a setup on a time frame, such as a five-minute chart, that catches your attention, drop down to smaller time frames, such as a one-or two-minute chart, to time your entries, exits, and stop placement.

- Be aware of the fact that securities that experience a large degree of overlap in prices from one bar to the next on a given time frame can make it more difficult to time entries and exits than those that do not.

- Different securities and sectors fall in and out of favor over time. Don't continue to doggedly pursue trades in a security that no longer gives you adequate returns on your investments. Move onto something where greater market participation is creating larger intraday and daily price movements and better follow-through.

- Begin to develop a set of guidelines for the types of trades you take so that you can start to categorize them. Strategies can also fall in and out of favor, depending on the overall trend development of the market. Classifying your strategies will allow you to more quickly locate the types of strategies that are working for you, and those that are not. Advanced analysis can even show you how when one particular strategy falls out of favor, it will most often be replaced by another on a consistent basis—such as how the failure of continuation patterns will start to indicate that it is time to begin to look for reversal strategies.

For more trading tips, go to www.traderslibrary.com/TLEcorner.

.

# FROM TRADE LOGS TO A TRADING JOURNAL

By touching upon the concept of labeling trades, we have begun to hit the limits of a trade log. Even though there are other data that you can track and include in a trade log, when you wish to understand the reasoning behind why things are they way they are, you have to go beyond mere measurements to a more in-depth system of analysis.

Trade logs are typically a form of electronic record-keeping. Even though I do know some traders that write them out manually, by tracking data in the form of an electronic spreadsheet, you are less likely to make errors. When approaching your performance from a journaling perspective, a little bit of good old-fashioned hands-on data analysis is still one of the best methods. This is particularly true when you move beyond some of the basics and delve more deeply into pattern and systems development, as well as the influences your emotions have upon your trading abilities.

# MY PERSONAL FAVORITE

Although I do use spreadsheets and other mediums to study my trades and overall performance, my favorite style of journal is a loose-leaf binder. When you are using a format such as a three-ring binder, you can easily organize and reorganize the components of your journal over time as your knowledge and skills grow and expand, making it particularly beneficial in the creation of strategy guides. You can also remove portions of the journal to make side-by-side comparisons much easier. I will often sit in the middle of my office floor with the charts I am studying spread out around me and search for similarities and differences in the data. Attempting to do this electronically would require more monitors than the average trader has available, although it is possible.

A lot of the problems traders run into stem from a lack of confidence in their system. This makes it easier to give in to emotions that may not have a very logical basis from the point of a successful trading system. When trading, the ability to think and act swiftly without hesitation is a major key to your success. The stronger your understanding of the technical side of trading, the easier it is to identify and overcome problems that relate to both technical and emotional issues. Therefore, let's begin with a focus upon technical analysis itself. By doing so, many of the other problem-causing areas should become greatly diminished or even eliminated.

When trading, the ability to think and act swiftly without hesitation is a major key to your success. The stronger your understanding of the technical side of trading, the easier it is to identify and overcome problems that relate to both technical and emotional issues.

## GETTING STARTED—GATHERING DATA

Approximately three weeks of trading data, or several dozen trades, is typically all it takes for most traders to have enough information to begin to analyze their trading style. As with a trade log, off-line versions of journaling can range from quite simple to very complex. Too much data can be overwhelming, so remember—start small and go from there.

The simplest form for a loose-leaf journal is as a collection of charts depicting the trades that an individual has executed. A lot of traders know that they should capture a screen shot of their trade, particularly if they used technical analysis to identify their setup. However, the image they capture is not always ideal for trade analysis. Individual setups may appear nearly identical on a smaller time frame, such as on a five-minute chart, but one setup may be successful while the other fails. Capturing an image of a five-minute chart alone may not allow the trader to determine the reasons for this difference. When you are looking at the components of any trade, you should consider both the large and small time frames.

## MULTIPLE TIME FRAMES

When I capture an image to print out for my trading journal, I enter the symbol for my trade on one of my monitors where a number of different time frames are displayed. When I day trade, my main chart for identifying the ideal time for a setup to develop is the five-minute chart. Nevertheless, I will also have a chart up for a one- or two-minute time frame, a 15-minute time frame, a 60-minute time frame, and a daily time frame. The larger time frames help me identify influential factors on a large scale that may impact my position, while the smaller time frames help find the optimal timing for entering or exiting a position.

## TICK CHARTS AND TIME FRAMES

Tick charts can be used in conjunction with, or in lieu of time frame charts. While a time frame chart tracks price changes in certain increments of time, such as one bar on a 15-minute chart representing the price range that occurred over the course of those 15 minutes, a tick chart will measure the price changes that take place over a certain number of trades. A 200-tick chart, for example, will show the price range over the course of 200 trades, or ticks.

## SCREEN SHOTS

Some charting platforms, when integrated with an execution platform, will allow you to mark where your entries and exits occurred within the charts. I like to take several screen shots of a setup as it unfolds. This allows me to study it from the initial moment of interest, to the moment of execution, to the time I exited the position, and finally to a shot captured after the security has played out past the time where I exited the position. This final screen shot will allow me to analyze whether or not the exit timing was done properly.

This final screen shot is one that all traders should capture for their journals even if they do not capture the others along the way. This can be done during slow times in the afternoon, if the setup occurred in the morning, or any time later in the evening. Even if you do not want to get into analyzing your trades quite yet, always include at least this step for every trade you take. As long as your entry and exit times and prices are marked on the charts, you can go back at any time and look at this data more thoroughly.

> If your charting software does not enter this information automatically, be sure to do so manually. It is quite a hassle to go back at a later date and try to line up the entry and exit times and prices from your account statements with where they took place on a chart.

## MARKING UP YOUR CHARTS

Many charting platforms will allow you to save a screen shot or print an image of your charts directly from the program. If yours does not allow you to do this, or does not offer the function to display your entry time and price on the charts, then you will need to use a supplementary program instead. There are a number of popular image editing programs available that you can use for this purpose. If you are running a computer with Windows installed, then you can use Microsoft Paint to do essentially the same thing you would if you were using a more expensive program. MS Paint is located under your start menu. Select "all programs" and then "accessories."

To capture and edit an image of your charts using Paint, first open the Paint program, and then minimize it to your systems tray. Make sure that your charts are fully visible on your monitor and then tap the Print Screen (PrtSc or PrtScn) button located on the upper right-hand side of a standard keyboard. Now restore the Paint program to your desktop and hold down the control (Ctrl) button, followed by the key for the letter "V." This will paste your screen shot into Paint. You can now use the Paint tools to draw on and annotate your charts.

Since the Print Screen button will have captured everything on all of your monitors, you may also need to trim down the image to display only the relevant charts. Use the "select" tool in the toolbar to select the portion of the image you wish to keep, and then go to Edit. Copy and paste that selection as a new image. Be sure to save your image along the way and always assign the image a name that will help you identify the type of strategy you used. For example, if you took a bull flag on a five-minute time frame at 9:45 EST in the ES on August 14th, 2009, you can name it *BullFlag5Min20090814ES945*. Although it may seem a bit wordy, this format will be invaluable when you begin to categorize and analyze your trades.

## TONI'S TIPS

### Chapter 6

- A simple three-ring binder is a great way to begin tracking your trades. Print out the charts depicting your trades with entry and exit points clearly marked. Then begin to group the trades according to similar strategies and traits.

- Screen shots of your trades to add to your journal should always include charts that depict the setup on multiple time frames. When two setups look the same on one time frame, yet one trade failed while the other succeeded, the cause is typically due to differences between them on the smaller or larger time frames.

- An easy way to "capture" the charts you have on your screen so that you can go back and review them is to hit the print screen key on your keyboard, open an image editing program, and save the screen shot in a folder devoted to your trading activity. Assign the image a name that includes some of the key details of the trade itself, such as the type of setup and time frame. This will make it easier to study them over time.

# TONI'S FIVE BUILDING BLOCKS OF PRICE DEVELOPMENT

Once you have completed at least a few dozen trades, the next step is to begin to make sense of the charts you have compiled. Most traders have a general idea of which trades were based upon similar concepts or patterns, but few have a system for analyzing those strategies and improving them.

When I first began to trade, I didn't have a solid plan either. I did notice, however, that winning positions and losing positions for setups that I attributed the same names to often had at least subtle differences in when and how they formed. These differences appeared to affect the probabilities and outcomes of the trades. They could either diminish the likelihood of success on the position, or they could diminish the potential reward for the trade when taken. Additionally, some traits made my strategies much more successful in certain situations than they were on average.

These characteristics, or building blocks of price development, seemed to fall into five categories. It is these five categories that I now use to assess all of my positions, and which serve as the tools I use to create and modify my trading systems.

**My five building blocks are:**

- Pace
- Support and resistance
- Trend development
- Volume
- Correction periods

As you can see, the labels are quite simple. Don't let that deceive you! These five tools are all that are used to build some of the most complex trading systems used by traders today. The more you understand them, the more useful they become for tweaking your own systems.

# PACE

The first building block is one that I call *pace*. Another word for it is *momentum*. Until I began teaching this component of price development in the late 1990s, most traders I came across had never considered it. Once it was pointed out, however, the typical response was, "I can't believe I never thought of that before!" When you are looking at pace in the context of a chart pattern, you are looking at how quickly the price of the security is changing over a specific amount of time as compared to the same increment of time in the past.

Examining pace can help you determine not only the upcoming price direction of a security, but also how quickly the next move in the security will take place. It can help you identify when a security is most likely to fall into a trading range, as well as whether that trading range will break higher or lower. It can also help you gauge the speed at which a price reversal is likely to occur and how far that reversal can go before it stalls.

Determining the pace of a move is a bit of a judgment call. There is no reason to try to use mathematical tools or formulas. Simply eyeballing past price action will suffice. What you are looking for is how quickly changes occur in the present compared to an average move in the past. When a security is trending higher, for example, think of it as a sliding scale from a very gradual ascent to an extreme one. Is the current move comparable to other rallies that fall in the middle of that sliding scale, or is it much slower or more rapid than in the past? How that climb compares to previous moves to the upside can help you determine how quickly the security will correct off its high when the rally comes to an end. It can help you decide whether or not to try to trade a reversal, or to wait for a congestive move and another continuation higher when that congestion breaks.

Figure 7.1 is a template that I created several years ago, and it has worked so well to teach this concept that I continue to use it to this day. It shows some of the most common ways that the pace of one move can affect the trend move that follows it. The sequence of the moves on this template is not important. Even though you will find securities that play out in this exact manner, as if the pace template is a pattern template, do not focus on it as such. Instead, take a look at how one move leads into the next and notice that when those moves accelerate or decelerate, they influence the subsequent move in the series. Subtle changes within a trend move on a smaller scale can be enough to impact the pace of the next move.

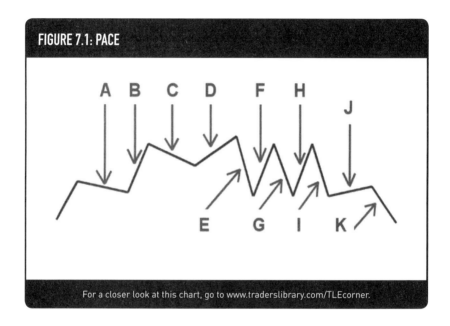

**FIGURE 7.1: PACE**

For a closer look at this chart, go to www.traderslibrary.com/TLEcorner.

**Key concepts to keep in mind are:**

- Faster-than-average moves will tend to correct with more gradual ones.

- Slower-than-average moves will typically be followed by more rapid ones.

- Those moves that create price action resembling a "V" or an upside-down "V" will more often develop into a longer trading range.

In Figure 7.1, the upside move labeled B was substantially stronger as it rallied than the pullback or correction labeled A had been on the downside. This meant that when the hypothetical security in this template began to correct from B's rally, it would have a higher chance of correcting or pulling back more gradually than it had rallied. When it pulled back in C, however, the pace of that correction was stronger than it had been in A. This shift in momentum affected the security's ability to rally as quickly as it had in B and led to a further change in pace on the upside in D. Now the upside pace was a lot slower and the security was creeping higher. Due to the slower overall upside pace, the odds increased that a breakdown from D would result in a stronger momentum on the downside, as seen in E.

Strong moves may not always lead to slower corrections. When a security rallies quickly, it can also reverse quickly and vice versa. This is what took place in E and F. The security fell sharply out of the slower upside move of D and then bounced quickly off lows to return to the zone from which it had broken. This created a "V" bottom. The result was an increased likelihood that the security would then fall into a trading range.

Although the momentum within a trading range does not always shift, when it does, it provides a strong indication for the direction in which the trading range will break. In the example of the trading range in my template, the pace shifts in J when it moves slowly higher at a pace much more gradual than the downside pace of I. This pointed to a breakdown out of the trading range as the most likely outcome of the range. When you are trading range breakouts, this knowledge can come in handy. This can be one of the things you look at if you develop a system for trading breakouts.

If you cannot see the changes in pace within a setup, drop down to a smaller time frame. Although a trading range may look like a series of bars overlapping each other in price on a bar or candlestick chart, if you drop down to a smaller time frame, or even switch from a time frame chart to a tick chart, you can more easily view the waves of back and forth action within the range itself.

Pace affects every strategy that is based upon technical analysis. When you flip through your charts to look for similarities and differences between your best and worst performing setups, it is one of the first things you should look at and compare. When I have a trade that does not work out, this is one of the most likely culprits. Even if the pace within a setup is ideal heading into a trade, if it does not react as anticipated, then it can provide clues for trade management to allow you to pull the most out of a position, or bail on the trade completely when necessary.

For example, if you took the bull flag labeled C in the template, then you may have expected an upside move comparable to the one labeled B because the pullback off the high, while stronger than the prior one, was still slower than average. When the security creeps higher instead, it can warn you that you will not likely receive the reward you had expected and you can adjust your stop or take gains more aggressively than you would have otherwise. You can even use it to reverse positions like when the move marked D breaks lower.

Examining pace can help you determine not only the upcoming price direction of a security, but also how quickly the next move in the security will take place. It is one of the first things you should look at and compare.

# SUPPORT AND RESISTANCE

A second building block for price development is the category of support and resistance levels. Support and resistance levels are price zones in a security that serve as barriers when a trend move is underway. When these price zones are underneath the current price of the security, they are called *support*. When they are overhead, they are called *resistance*. Sometimes these barriers are temporary and a security can test that level, pull back only slightly, and then push through it. At other times, these price zones can be strong enough to lead to more substantial price reversals.

## TYPES OF SUPPORT AND RESISTANCE

There are a number of different types of support and resistance levels. They fall into two broader categories: *price* support and resistance levels, and *indicator* support and resistance levels. Price support and resistance levels are based purely upon the visible action within the security. These include levels such as whole numbers, previous highs and lows, and the security's closing price at the end of a session. You can identify these zones without any tool other than the charts themselves.

Support and resistance levels can also be calculated using additional data not easily visualized by the untrained eye. Instead, the relationships between price and volume are calculated mathematically and used to predict the levels that will stall or reverse a security's price action. Some of these relationships will reveal the most ideal time of the day or day of the week for a setup to trigger coming out of a period of congestion, where a security has been bouncing back and forth between price support and resistance levels.

## MOVING AVERAGES

A moving average is a good example of an indicator that can help time your entry and exit triggers on trading range breakouts. Moving averages show the average value of a security's price over time. This average is plotted as a line on the chart in question. One of the most popular moving averages is the 20-period moving average. This measures the average closing price of the last 20 time frame increments on a chart. If you are examining a 20-period moving average on a 15-minute chart, then the moving average would be based upon the average closing price of the previous 20 increments of 15 minutes each. These moving averages can serve as support or resistance levels even when a security has fallen into a trading range, because it can take time for the moving average to catch up. Once the moving average has caught up to the current price level, then that moving average will serve as support in the case of prices moving higher overall, or resistance if prices are trending lower. These levels will often act as a catalyst to jump-start a breakout from the congestion.

Moving averages can also serve as support or resistance for securities already on the move. I usually use a 20- and 200-period moving average on my intraday charts. The 200 does not get as much use for timing trades as the 20 does, but I do use it a great deal. It can help time larger reversals as well as serve as a good level for setting targets.

Figure 7.2 depicts a five-minute time frame of the Diamonds (DIA), which is the Dow Jones Industrial Average's tracking stock—a type of ETF. The 20-period moving average serves as a resistance zone as prices fall in the DIA, but after the reversal at noon, the DIA breaks this moving average resistance. It then becomes support throughout the afternoon uptrend whenever the

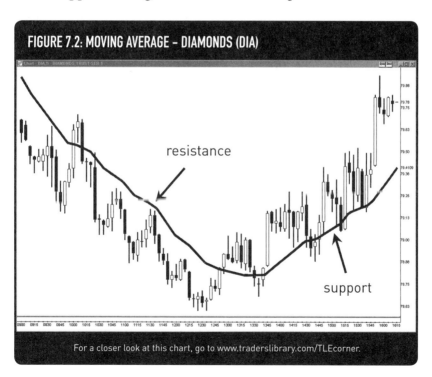

FIGURE 7.2: MOVING AVERAGE – DIAMONDS (DIA)

For a closer look at this chart, go to www.traderslibrary.com/TLEcorner.

security pulls back or bases sideways into it. Notice that by bouncing off the moving average at the exact moment it touches, the price action does not hold perfectly. The zone of the moving average, however, held each and every time until the trend reversed. It would not have been at all uncommon to have seen the 200-period moving average stall these five-minute trends as either the midday reversal zone support at noon, or resistance to trigger the end of the afternoon rally.

There are many other popular indicators in use today, and there are quite a few places that can serve as potential price support and resistance levels. If you look hard enough, you can find support or resistance on at least one time frame, which will create or contribute to every pause or minor correction within a security. In order to make support and resistance levels more useful in trade analysis, you should keep two things in mind:

- The larger the time frame a support or resistance level forms on, the stronger that level will be.

- When multiple forms of support or resistance converge in a single price zone, that zone will serve as a much stronger support or resistance level than it would have with just one type of support or resistance hitting at that time.

# TREND DEVELOPMENT

My third building block of price development is an examination of trend development, or the placement of a setup, entry, or exit within a larger trend move. When a trader locates a setup on one time frame that looks nearly identical to a setup he traded in the past on the same time frame—except that the newer setup fails while the other succeeded—then the most common culprit is the difference in where the setup took place within the larger trend. If you do not step back to examine multiple time frames, then this is very easy to overlook. This is why it is always important to include a record of what additional time frames looked like when you copy chart images into your journal. You may not recognize these differences in the beginning, but the more examples you have of a strategy, the more you will start to identify even the most subtle differences from one trade to the next.

## FLAGS AND BREAKOUTS

Flag patterns and breakouts are two of the most widely popular *and* misunderstood setups. In my own trading journal, I treat flags and breakouts as the same pattern because the building blocks that create a favorable bull flag are almost identical to those that create a strong upside breakout from a sideways trading range. The only difference is that a bull flag has a slight downward slant to its correction, whereas the trading range corrects in more of a sideways manner.

Trends will often form in waves of three and two, with primary trends having three waves of buying or selling, and corrective trend moves having two waves. For instance, an uptrend move will often consist of three pushes higher that are broken up with two smaller trend moves lower in between each of the larger upside ones. A typical template for this type of action can be seen in Figure 7.3. In the corrective moves, as shown with the smaller numbers, the waves of correction can take place primarily through time or through price. This will lead to flags, bases, or triangles within the larger trend.

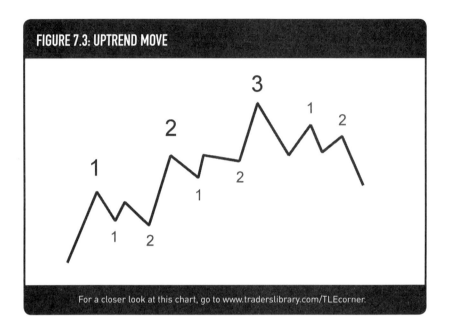

FIGURE 7.3: UPTREND MOVE

For a closer look at this chart, go to www.traderslibrary.com/TLEcorner.

One of the main misconceptions traders have is that any gradual pullback in an uptrend is a bull flag. Another misconception is that trading ranges most commonly break in the direction of the larger trend. Not every pullback or base along highs in an uptrend offers a strong buying opportunity, though. If a larger uptrend is exhausted, which is typically the case if it has already had three pushes higher, then attempts to push the trend even further can be easily thwarted. This can lead to false entry signals, more plentiful stop losses, and reduced rewards—even when the security moves far enough in the desired direction to no longer risk a loss. Newer trends will tend to offer the best continuation patterns, but more extended trends can start to favor the development of reversal patterns instead.

A trader needs to combine the five building blocks in order to understand how they work together within a pattern. This will allow traders to determine whether or not a pattern still has room to make it worthwhile for a faster trade in the direction of the larger trend, or whether it is more favorable to monitor for a reversal pattern. If the pace on each of the waves of buying in an uptrend is slower than the one that preceded it, then the chances are greater that a third pullback off the third wave of upside would serve as a reversal trigger. Figure 7.4 displays the template I used for pace. You can see that this would be the case if the move labeled D was the third wave higher in the trend. It would trigger a short if it breaks.

On the other hand, if the pace is steady on the upside each time and the pullback off the third high is still slower than average,

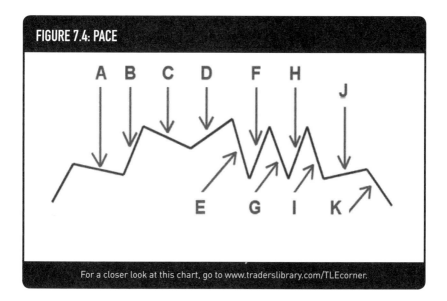

**FIGURE 7.4: PACE**

For a closer look at this chart, go to www.traderslibrary.com/TLEcorner.

then the security can more easily attempt at least a retest of that
third high, sometimes even break it slightly, before creating a reversal pattern. In this case, the security offers not only a small
continuation pattern, but then develops into a reversal pattern.
In the pace template, an example of this would be if the move
marked B was the third push higher in the trend. Figure 7.5 of
Comerica, Inc. (CMA) shows this action in reverse. It comes off
the third low and then attempts a fourth one, but instead, it hugs
the 40-period simple moving average into February 2009 and only
manages a very slight lower low before breaking above the moving
average in March.

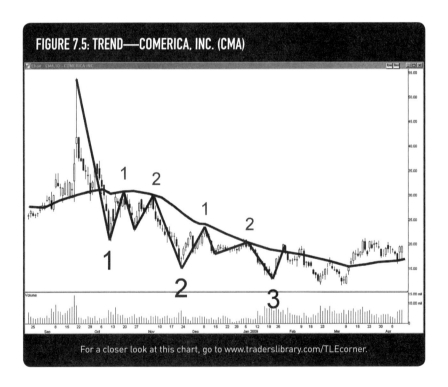

FIGURE 7.5: TREND—COMERICA, INC. (CMA)

For a closer look at this chart, go to www.traderslibrary.com/TLEcorner.

Support and resistance levels will also work together with trend development. If the trend is in a new downtrend, then resistance such as the 40-period moving average in Comerica, Inc. (CMA) in Figure 7.5 can serve as a strong price zone for timing entries on pullbacks such as bear flags. If a security attempts to trigger this type of setup without first testing a resistance level, then there is a greater chance of a false trigger. Price action could then pull back up for a stronger test of resistance before attempting to break lower again. This was the case when CMA first bounced off the second low in the larger downtrend at the end of November 2007. Locating the resistance levels for a correction is thus an important clue for timing an entry point.

As we've seen, support and resistance levels can assist in timing the continuation moves within a trend. They can also stall trend moves, or even reverse them. When support levels come together at lows at the same time that a trend pushes lower on its third leg down, these support levels will help call an end to that move. As such, identifying the support and resistance levels ahead of time can provide clues for how difficult it may be to achieve your goals, and can help you time your exits.

> A trader needs to combine the five building blocks in order to understand how they work together within a pattern.

# VOLUME

Volume is my fourth building block. You can more easily gauge participation levels in a security when you keep an eye on the number of shares or contracts that exchange hands within a given increment of time. This is the volume, and it is often displayed as a line or bar chart underneath the main chart, which depicts the security's overall price action. Changes in volume within a move can help you identify the best times to enter new positions, as well as when to get out. How you read volume is often a matter of where the price action is in the larger trend and the pace of the price moves. As you develop strategies, watch how volume influences the success or failure of your trades.

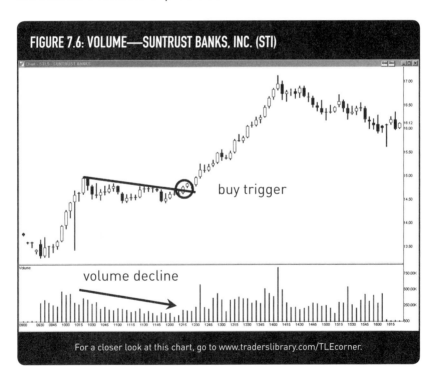

FIGURE 7.6: VOLUME—SUNTRUST BANKS, INC. (STI)

For a closer look at this chart, go to www.traderslibrary.com/TLEcorner.

One example of volume within the formation of a setup is during the creation of a bull flag or upper level base, such as the gradual correction in SunTrust Banks, Inc. (STI) in Figure 7.6. Assuming that it is placed in the middle of a larger trend, and that there is no strong overhead resistance in the immediate vicinity, volume can provide you with another clue for how successful your trade will be. In this type of pattern, you ideally want to see volume decreasing as the flag forms into support. This shows a lack of participation by the sellers. If volume picks up strongly following the breakout from the flag, then it will help confirm the setup and indicate that it has a good chance of moving into upper target levels.

# CORRECTION PERIODS

The fifth thing that I consider when placing or exiting a trade is the category for the correction periods in the market. Correction periods are times of the day or times of the year where an individual security or the overall market is most likely to correct from a previous trend move or begin a new one. If an uptrend is in play heading into a correction period, then the odds increase that the security can run into its own glass ceiling. This can lead to a pullback off highs for a correction in price, or force the security into a trading range for a correction over time. Most are a combination of both and are highly influenced by the pace of the move that takes place immediately prior to the correction period.

There are quite a few different correction periods and their importance depends upon your particular time frame, as well as the type of security that you trade. If you are a day trader, then one of the main correction periods takes place at 14:00 (or 2:00 pm EST). Breakouts and flags that form on 15-minute time frames will often trigger at this time zone. Pivots off highs and lows that mark the end of a trend move are also very common. The breakout that we examined in STI in Figure 7.6 ran into resistance at this particular correction period, bringing an end to the strong uptrend intraday displayed in Figure 7.7.

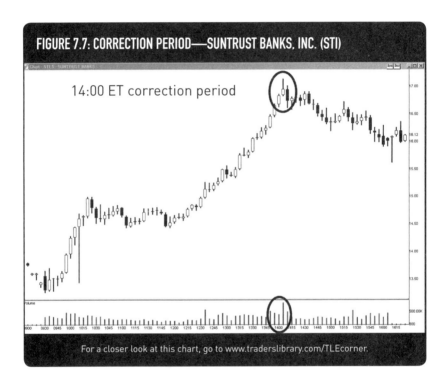

FIGURE 7.7: CORRECTION PERIOD—SUNTRUST BANKS, INC. (STI)

14:00 ET correction period

For a closer look at this chart, go to www.traderslibrary.com/TLEcorner.

# USE THE BUILDING BLOCKS TOGETHER

Each of the five building blocks I have shared is an integral part of developing strategies in the market. The tricky part is learning how to read them as individual components and to cultivate an understanding of the interplay between them. Such a feat is impossible without the use of a journal. You may get help from someone that already has a strong set of skills to help get you started and make the journey easier, but every trader has a different set of skills and will need to use these building blocks differently to personalize their market approach. As a result, even a qualified trading coach is going to require access to your trade journal if they plan to work with you within the context of your own skill set.

In my *Trading Made Simple* series, I walk through each of these five building blocks one at a time, and in much greater detail than I have touched upon here. Visit www.tonihansen.com if you are in search of more information. These tools will serve as the foundation for any serious trade analysis from a technical perspective.

# TONI'S TIPS

## Chapter 7

- Price patterns in the market can be distinguished from one another by examining the components, or building blocks, of the patterns themselves. My five building blocks of price development are pace, support and resistance, trend development, volume, and correction periods. Each of these should be examined in turn when analyzing a past or potential trade.

- Although I look at each of the five building blocks when trading, I have found that pace and trend placement or trend development have the greatest impact upon the outcome of a trade. Always pay very close attention to these two traits, because they can either make or break a setup.

- Focus on new trends for continuation patterns and trends that have already had three waves of buying or selling for reversal patterns. Be sure to also watch the pace within the trend moves themselves to support your bias.

For more trading tips, go to www.traderslibrary.com/TLEcorner.

# 8

# BUILDING A SUCCESSFUL STRATEGY

Many traders come into the markets thinking that topics such as support and resistance and volume are rather basic and straightforward, but the impact that each of my building blocks has on price development depends upon how they fit together. For example, high volume on an extended downtrend can indicate something quite different than high volume at the start of a new downtrend. While the former often provides confirmation of trend exhaustion and the impending end to a downtrend move that had gained momentum throughout, the latter can confirm the beginning of a new downtrend, where the most rapid descent will take place at the beginning of the trend. High volume on an extended downtrend, however, does not always signal that prices will begin to immediately reverse.

The pace of the selling, the placement of support levels, and when the next correction period takes place will all create either pros or cons in favor of when the low of the selloff will actually hold. The closer the price is to a strong support level, and the closer it is to a correction period, the higher the odds are that the low will be established. The pace of the selloff will then affect how rapidly it pulls up off those lows or whether it just falls into a range.

Within each strategy that you develop, you will need to pay attention to these characteristics to judge the odds on your position.

# VISUALIZING THE BUILDING BLOCKS

The first thing that I do after I print out the charts for one of my trades is to go through and mark it up according to how the five building blocks have affected the price action. Although this can be done electronically using Paint or another image editing platform, I prefer pencils, pens, and markers. They are simply faster for me to use than drawing and annotating my charts using a software program. Although I will keep an electronic back-up of my charts on my computer, I print out the charts for each trade and keep them in a loose-leaf binder for analysis. I typically only edit charts on my computer when I am creating them for others to view. If you do wish to keep copies of your charts digitally as well, then you can still analyze them manually and scan the marked-up charts back onto your computer.

How much or how little information you wish to include on your charts is up to you. There are a couple of approaches you can take. The first is a very simplistic approach whereby you take one of the building blocks at a time and focus on it across each of your trades, making notes on how that building block impacted your results.

For example, look at how each trade performed in relation to the correction periods. This would be one of the easiest to start with, and you can develop rules based upon your best and worst performers. This will tie into the time-of-day analysis that was also made possible through the use of a trade log. One result of this analysis could be the decision to only take trades that trigger coming out of specific correction periods. You could also reduce your exposure on those that do not meet these criteria and increase your position size on the ones that do meet your criteria.

Each of the five building blocks can be analyzed in such a manner, but the analysis of correction periods will be easiest, since with the other four, you will be working with multiple variables. It is further complicated if you trade multiple types of setups.

## ANALYSIS BY TYPE OF SETUP

There is another approach for analyzing charts using the five building blocks that addresses these concerns. You will want to go through your trades and pull out the ones that you feel fit into a specific category, such as all bull flags. Although checking out the correlation between correction periods and your trades is a quick way to pick out at least one trait in your trading to focus upon or modify, I prefer this second method for more in-depth analysis.

Focusing by types of setups is more precise than looking at volume moves on every one of your trades and then trying to understand how it affects your trading overall. Instead, you can focus on volume as well as the other building blocks one at a time, or as a larger picture within the context of just one pattern. To make this process simpler, one of the first things I did when I began to keep a journal like this was to divide my binder into different segments according to the types of setups I was trading. Within each segment, I put the winning trades at the beginning of the section and the losing ones at the end. This makes it very easy to pull out the charts I wish to look at more closely to advance my skills on a particular strategy.

I don't worry much about the chronological order of the trades in my journal. If I discover a setup that doesn't quite fit the mold I have created, then I move it to another category. I have one segment of my journal where I place trades that I cannot seem to fit into any of my main categories. At times, I will start to recognize similarities and move them into their own section, but many times these end up being trades I took on a whim without enough real evidence to have backed them up as solid strategies. What's good about these anomaly trades is they can be used to identify cracks in my approach to the markets. Every trader I know ends up with trades that fall into a "What was I thinking?" category.

I still segment trades in this manner, but these days my journal is more a collection of journals, where each strategy has its own binder that is partitioned into variations of those strategies.

To help make this type of system's analysis easier, when I print out the charts for a trade, I write the name that I assign to a strategy in pencil in the upper right corner with a red arrow for a short and a green arrow for a long. Underneath that, I will note the time frame that was the main focus for my trade. By using pencil I can go back at a later date and rename it, or narrow down the name to something more specific as I develop my system and start to analyze the variations within the different strategies.

# DIGGING IN

Once you pick out a strategy to focus upon, the next step is to make your way through each of the five building blocks. Draw on your charts to make specific points stand out. An example of this can been seen in Figure 9.1 in the next chapter, where I discuss a bear flag that took place in the ES. A ruler works well to help show off the support and resistance levels and the pace of move, as well as to make the relevant correction periods more visible. Be sure that your drawings do not overpower the depiction of the price action itself. Pale colors, fine-tipped markers, and highlighters work best. If you cannot see the price action in order to study it, it can be difficult to recognize similarities between trades when they begin to unfold in the future. It is also helpful to use the same colors throughout your journal to point out similar traits.

Try to keep space available on the page when you print out your charts. Wider margins will provide you with the room to jot down notes and annotate the charts themselves. If you want, print out the charts on two pages with the smaller time frame that you used to time the entry and exits on one page, and the supplemental charts depicting the trade's location in the larger time frames on another page.

The next step is to create a list of traits based upon the five building blocks. Create a heading for each and then describe as simply as possible what you see as it relates to each specific building block. Keep in mind that some of the categories will have multiple qualities.

For example, if you start with trend development, you can describe the placement of the trade in both larger and smaller time frames. Every setup will also have multiple support and resistance levels. A buy setup may run into a support level just prior to setting up. It may also have a number of resistance levels that converged in one area overhead that affected its ability to push higher.

This list has the potential of becoming quite long, so instead of listing every little thing, focus upon the traits that led you to make your decisions when executing the trade from start to finish. Then write down anything that stands out as something you missed taking note of or failed to consider as a strong trait when you took the trade, but you can see afterwards that it affected the price development within the security. Other traits will start to stand out over time, but you can always go back and reexamine your trades.

## EXAMPLE LIST

My style of journaling has not changed much over the years. Figure 8.1 depicts a journal entry on a buy setup I took back in 2006 in First Cash Financial Services, Inc. (FCFS). The top chart is a one-minute time frame and displays the entry and exit timing on the position. It also has a couple of notes regarding my thoughts on

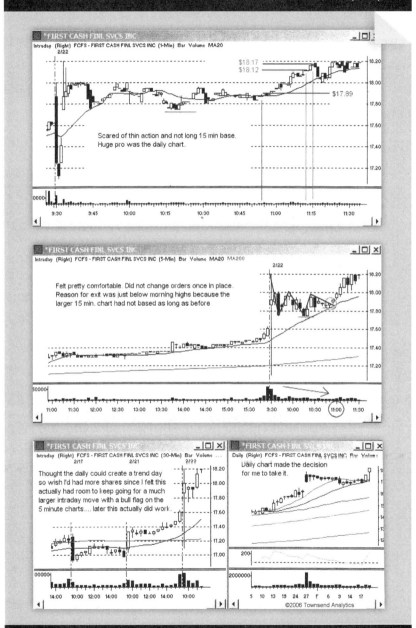

**FIGURE 8.1: JOURNAL ENTRY – FIRST CASH FINANCIAL SERVICES, INC. (FCFS)**

Scared of thin action and not long 15 min base.
Huge pro was the daily chart.

Felt pretty comfortable. Did not change orders once in place.
Reason for exit was just below morning highs because the
larger 15 min. chart had not based as long as before

Thought the daily could create a trend day
so wish I'd had more shares since I felt this
actually had room to keep going for a much
larger intraday move with a bull flag on the
5 minute charts.... later this actually did work.

Daily chart made the decision
for me to take it.

©2006 Townsend Analytics

For a closer look at these charts, go to www.traderslibrary.com/TLEcorner.

the trade. Underneath it is the five-minute chart, which was the primary time frame that my strategy developed on.

If we were to go through this trade and list the characteristics that stand out from the perspective of the five building blocks and make guesses as to which traits may be the most influential on the outcome of the setup, it could look a lot like this:

**Trend Development:**

- Breakout on a daily time frame with a modest gap approximately the size of an average day's range.

- Opening gap is second wave of upside on the daily breakout.

- Intraday FCFS had two waves of pullback within the morning triangle, followed by a third pullback to extend the triangle.

- The intraday base on the 21st is shorter than the intraday base the morning of the 22nd.

**Support and Resistance:**

- Daily breakout comes off the 20-day simple moving average (sma) support.

- Opening gap breaks FCFS out of daily range and over previous highs with no immediately strong daily resistance.

- $18.00 opening whole price resistance.

- Opening gap completes equal move on the 15-minute time frame, leading to resistance at the open.

- Five-minute, 20-sma serves as support on the second and third corrective moves off intraday highs in the opening triangle.

**Pace:**

- Daily breakout from slower, downside-paced congestion leads to stronger-than-average upside momentum.
- Pace is stronger than average on the upside into the open intraday as well.
- Pace within the opening triangle shifts with slower downside on each correction off highs.

**Volume:**

- Volume declined and then fell flat in the daily congestion.
- Volume out of the open the day of the gap was stronger than average.
- Volume during the intraday trading range drops off compared to the start of the range.

**Correction Periods:**

- Daily breakout takes place in the second half of February.
- Second low in the range corresponds to 10:15 ET.
- Third low in the range corresponds to 10:45 ET.
- Breakout from the intraday range takes place at approximately 11:00 ET.
- Resistance at morning highs hits at 11:15 ET.

All of the above observations are mere statements of facts. In and of themselves they do not represent any particular strategy. The impact they have on the success of the breakout will be unknown to an amateur, but over time, some of the traits may continue to surface from one setup to the next and suggest that setups with these traits will have higher odds of success. Other traits, however, may prove to be unhelpful in structuring a strategy.

# IT'S ALL IN THE GUESS WORK

Going from merely listing the characteristics of a setup to developing a system for recognizing how these building blocks come together to impact the trade's development takes some time. You must be patient with the process.

It is necessary to first collect enough samples of the particular strategy you are trying to analyze, such as a bull flag. Then, you have to make the time to reflect upon the characteristics of the successful strategies and compare them to the characteristics of those that failed. This requires going through each of the five building blocks one by one and creating lists of common traits amongst the most successful and least successful trades taken using the same strategy. These will help you create templates and strategy guidelines for future trades that are comprised of pros, cons, and neutral characteristics of a setup.

For example, in Figure 8.1, the 20-period simple moving average (sma) in FCFS was support at the time of my entry coming out of the 11:00 ET correction period. It also had two waves of correction and was forming a third wave at a more gradual pace with declining volume on the second test of the 20-period sma. All of these are highly favorable traits for a breakout buy setup. This pattern was similar on the daily time frame shown in the lower right. The intraday trigger corresponded to a daily trigger off the 20-day sma on a gap higher. This same compilation of building blocks has proven consistently successful for me over the past decade when approaching breakouts, so when I am searching for setups, I look for these criteria as favorable qualities with a developing breakout formation.

Other traits, such as the fact that FCFS broke out in the second half of February, have so far proven less helpful in gauging their own impact upon the outcome of the trade. If a trader saw a lot of successful breakouts taking place at this same time period year after year, then they could conclude that this is a correction period in the market and idyllic for entry timing. My own studies, however, suggest that January and March are more common than February for such moves, so the weekly or monthly timing in this case is not a pro for the setup. Nevertheless, it is not necessarily a con either, unless it can be proven that over the years there are many more breakouts that fail in February than in other months.

## DRAWING CONCLUSIONS

So, don't be afraid to make guesses when you are studying your trades. A large part of developing a strategy is utilizing the data you have and reflecting upon that data to draw conclusions about how certain traits affect the outcome of a position. By examining trades after the fact, a trader can typically go back and look at their positions with greater objectivity than while a position is being played out.

## LOOKING BACK

Despite the cliché, hindsight is not always twenty-twenty. Although after the fact we might think it was silly that we didn't act according to certain instincts, this doesn't mean we fully comprehend why something felt instinctive in the first place. Without a reason, it is sometimes difficult to have the confidence to follow our intuition. By returning to our trades through our journals, you can compare the trades you felt strongly about and yet failed to act upon to others that appear similar in nature. You can then attempt to comprehend the root causes contributing to the beginning or end of a price move. This does not mean that your first assumption for why a security acted in the way that it did will be the correct one. Nor does it mean that there are not other characteristics that you have failed to recognize that may also be affecting the way the price action played out within a position.

# TESTING THEORIES, BUILDING STRATEGIES

Professionals in many areas of science, including archaeology, utilize a system for testing out their theories which involves considering each theory's ability to be falsified. A theory is falsifiable if it can be *proven* false through observation or experimentation. When it comes to developing a trading system based on the five building blocks, all theories are falsifiable because it takes just one exception to disprove it. Of course, all traders know that perfection is not possible, so we seek to come as close to it as we can. By examining theories that have been proven false, we can direct our focus and attempt to understand why they did not hold true. This allows us to modify or replace them with theories that explain the aberrations found in our previous theory. Over time, this leads to a complex understanding of price action.

One example of an observation that a trader might make that is falsifiable is: "During all trading ranges, it is necessary for volume to decline within the range in order to allow the security to show strong follow-through on a breakout from that range in the direction of the trend." Even though this may have been the case throughout most of the trades an individual takes, and it serves as a good starting point for developing a strategy, it is not a *true* statement. At times, volume will decline within a trading range, but the breakout will be weak and will quickly fail. In other cases, a security may be forming a solid trading range and not experience much of a volume decline, yet it still breaks strongly out of the range.

By examining the exceptions to the theory, in which it was proven false, a trader can begin to understand the other components that go into creating a strong trading range breakout in which declining volume plays a role. For example, the theory that "a decline in volume within a trading range, whereby the trading range occurs in the beginning stages of a new trend, will increase the odds of a strong follow-through on a breakout in the direction of the trend" is more accurate.

Even though a trading range may develop with light volume, if the trend is extended, there will be a higher incidence of failure on the part of a breakout attempting to sustain itself in the direction of that trend. This can easily prevent a trader from obtaining the types of gains they would typically see from a breakout occurring earlier in a trend. Furthermore, this revised statement no longer makes the volume decline a necessary component to create a strong range breakout, but rather one that plays a supporting role.

## WEIGHING THE PROS AND CONS

As each of the building blocks becomes incorporated within a theory, strategies begin to emerge. Within those strategies, certain characteristics of the five building blocks become either pros or cons for achieving a desirable outcome on a position. Certain traits will affect the chances that a position will succeed, while others will determine the level of that success. Additionally, certain traits will weigh more heavily on the level of success than others.

While the demonstration of a trait may prove to be a pro and help a setup succeed, the absence of that trait may not prove detrimental to the setup. For example, although a breakout from a trading range may be extremely favorable when volume declines within the range, the lack of a volume decline throughout the range may not affect the odds of it achieving a successful outcome to the trade all the time. On the other hand, an increase in volume might prove more harmful.

Further examination of our theory on the effect of volume on the outcome of a trading range breakout can reveal things such as the fact that volume typically increases towards the end of the regular trading session. As a result, trading ranges occurring at these times may not experience a decrease in volume, but will instead experience volume activity that is more consistent from one bar to the next on a given time frame such as the five-minute chart. Since volume typically increases at that time of the day, however, the fact that volume fails to increase within a trading range that forms during this time period may not be a con, but rather serves as the equivalent of a volume decline.

This will further amend our previous theory and lead to a new one such as, "a decline in volume within a trading range, whereby the trading range that occurs in the beginning stages of a new trend *and prior to the final hour of trade,* will increase the odds of a strong follow-through on a breakout in the direction of the trend."

# MARKET TIMING GUIDE

As I develop strategies for trading, I create lists of pros and cons for those strategies. This led me to create a supplement to my trading journal that I call my *Market Timing Guide.* In it I list my most common strategies, and how they are impacted by my five building blocks. In the version of the guide that I created for my clients, I show several examples of each strategy with the pros and cons listed below sample trades fitting those categories. In my own journals, the description is followed by each of the trades I've taken that fall into that particular category.

An example of one of the strategies in my Market Timing Guide is how I trade a breakout buy. The core traits of this particular setup according to my own style of market analysis are shown below.

## Breakout Buy Setup

**Description:** Also called a "rectangle," this pattern is based upon a sideways trading range breaking higher. It is most commonly traded as a continuation pattern, which is then called a consolidation. But a sideways range can at times also break in the direction opposite of the trend that had been in place heading into the trading range. In this description, the traits will be discussed as if they are in a continuation buy setup, but they can easily be reversed in order to use them in a short setup.

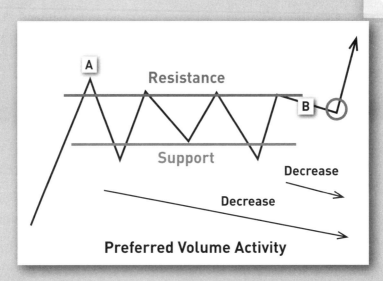

**Criteria:** The criteria for a rectangular breakout pattern from a sideways trading range is very similar to a triangle range breakout. Most of the same criteria, as well as the pros and cons will apply. The difference is that there are more comparable highs and lows, as opposed to a narrowing range or trend channel. There must be at least two highs and two lows within the range to identify it as a trading range if there is back and forth action. If there is just a lot of overlap from one bar to the next, then these waves of buying and selling will be more difficult to discern.

**Entry:** There are several entry techniques that work well on this pattern.

The technique which is the most widely taught is to draw a line connecting the highs of the range to each other and another line connecting the lows of the range. In the case of an upside range breakout, the trigger would occur when that upper trend line breaks higher. This is one of the least preferred methods to entering a breakout, second only to taking a breakout from the absolute highs of the range.

Another method in the case of a buy setup is to enter above the previous high after at least two highs are established.

A third setup, which is the one that will generate the highest reward compared to risk, is to watch the moves within the range and monitor the pace of each move. When the security pulls back more gradually off the highs than before, or hugs the upper trend line, use a break higher from that smaller downtrend or sideways trend within the larger trading range for an entry trigger.

**Stop:** Under the last pivot low within the range, or if it bases on a smaller time frame within the larger trend channel, then a stop can be placed under the lows of that smaller range. Use greater caution when keeping a tighter stop such as this if the security is very volatile, meaning there is a lot of back and forth action and overlap even as it trends, if the pace has yet to change within the range when it breaks, or if the security is thinly traded.

**Target:** The targets on a breakout will depend upon whether they are continuations or reversals of the previous trend.

- In the case of a continuation buy pattern, when the pace or momentum on the breakout move is comparable to that of the move heading into the trading range itself then a target is an equal or measured move. This involves taking the move into the range, from the lows of that move to the highs at the start of the range, and then comparing that to the lows at the start of the breakout and projecting them higher. If the momentum is slower than the previous rally, then it will be more difficult to hit that equal move and it will be necessary to identify closer resistance levels. If the momentum is stronger than that previous move, then a larger than equal move can form.

- When the breakout from the range is a reversal pattern off lows, however, then monitor the price and moving average resistance levels overhead. If a downtrend preceded the base at lows and then turned around and headed higher, then the level at which a previous bear flag broke lower would be resistance and a strong initial target, as would a resistance level such as a 200-period simple moving average, although any number of major moving averages can come into play on multiple time frames to serve as resistance. The resistance will be much stronger if several resistance levels are hitting at about the same time.

## Ideal Traits for Toni's Five Building Blocks on a Breakout from a Trading Range

**Pace:** As a trading range begins, it is common for the initial downside move(s) to be average or stronger than average. As the range progresses, however, the odds are highest when the pullbacks from the highs are more gradual than the upside moves within the range. A base near the highs of the range or move with only a very slight downside slant off the upper end of the range is preferred.

**Volume:** Watch for declining volume throughout the pattern's development, with higher volume on the upside moves within the range and lighter volume on the downside as the pattern progresses. The best ones are when the volume is at its lightest level of the day, just prior to the breakout, as it bases at highs or pulls back gradually (in the case of a day trade).

**Correction Periods:** It is ideal when the last pivot low within the range, or the breakout from the range occurs at the same time as a correction period.

**Support/Resistance:**

- As a continuation pattern, this setup is most ideal when it forms into the uptrend line on a larger trend, or moving average support such as a 20-period sma. Check to see if that level was also support on a previous correction, or if this is the first correction in a new uptrend; then look to see what the previous moving average resistance level was that broke to create the first higher high.

- If there is strong resistance on a larger time frame, such as the range forming intraday on a 15-minute time frame, and there is a 50-day sma overhead that will be hitting for the first time in the trend move, then that level will have a more difficult time breaking. The same is true if it forms on a five-minute chart and has a five-minute 200 sma shortly overhead.

**Trend Placement/Trend Development:** A breakout is typically considered to be a continuation pattern, but can also be a reversal pattern.

- As a continuation pattern, it is best if the uptrend has only one or two waves of upside.

- As a reversal pattern, it helps if the pace of each of the downside moves in the previous downtrend is slower than the one that preceded it, and that there were three waves of selling within that downtrend.

- A typical breakout tends to take place on the third or fourth test of the upper trend line for the trading range.

(copyright 2007-2009 Toni Hansen)

To facilitate analysis of your trades over time, try to keep the order of the pros and cons you list similar from one trade to the next. For instance, begin with trend development, followed by the support and resistance levels, pace, volume, and finally the correction periods. You do not have to use this particular order, but by keeping them organized in the same manner throughout your journal, you can more easily locate the action you wish to compare without having to read through the description of the entire trade.

## EXCEPTIONS CAN BECOME THE RULES

Under each of the pros and cons at the beginning of each section of your journal, you should also keep a list of exceptions to the rules that you have laid out, as well as a few "maybes" based upon your guesses for how certain traits may impact price action. Over time, the exceptions may become strategies of their own. These may not end up being strategies that you choose to trade; instead they may be situations where you *avoid* a trade.

## WHEN TO STAY OUT OF A TRADE

This is another reason a trading journal is so important to your success. A trading journal will help you explore alternative solutions to different problems or situations. The choice to stay on the sidelines is one that many traders may not consider. An important concept for any trader to learn early on, however, is that cash itself is a position. So when certain elements line up, instead of favoring the initiation of a trade, they may signal that the best position is to wait until that current phase within the security passes.

# PASSIVE ANALYSIS TO ACTIVE ANALYSIS

The well-known financial historian, economist, and educator Peter Bernstein stated that, "in a sense, conjecture is the process of estimating the whole from the parts." The beginning phase of developing a trading system is conjecture at its finest. A trader starts by speculating on which traits may have the greatest influence upon the outcome of current price action, and then uses this guesswork as a framework for further analysis.

Focusing upon the aftermath of a trade, however, is only part of the process. A trading system is only as good as your ability to implement it. Many traders make top-notch analysts, but struggle to pull consistent gains from their own accounts. I struggled with this for quite a while myself. Even though I would enter a position based upon the guidelines I created using the style of analysis I described earlier, inevitably I would fail to follow that plan. There was no logical reason for this failing from a technical standpoint. What it came down to was the impact my emotions were having upon my success.

## NOT YOUR LITTLE SISTER'S DIARY

A journal is very helpful in identifying the trigger points within a trade where your emotions can take over and override your positive programming and system of carefully constructed guidelines. This is where taking multiple screen shots comes into play, as well as the introduction of another type of journal: the notebook. This is a journal in the most traditional sense.

When many of us think of "keeping a journal," we are often think-ing along the lines of a diary or personal account of our daily lives. Of course, I would bet that more of my female readers would relate to this than the men. Nevertheless, perhaps those of you of the opposite sex can remember stealing your sister's diary in an act of mischief. Well, this more intimate form of record-keeping can play a vital role in helping you overcome a lot of the road blocks you may face when you implement your trading system.

## DOUBT IS A BAD DRIVER

I mentioned earlier that it is ideal to take several screen shots of your trades as they progress, from the moment they first capture your attention to a time far enough past your exit to be able to view the immediate aftermath. The point in doing so is to capture those moments in time, without the benefit of hindsight, to allow you to focus more clearly upon the aspects of a setup that you grasp well, as opposed to those where you still feel a great deal of doubt. When we do not stick to our plan on a particular strategy, it is most likely because doubt has crept in and regained control. I don't know about you, but Doubt is not who I would like behind the wheel when I'm in a trade.

Typically, the first image of a trade I capture is within seconds of entering the position. It is very easy to hit the Print Screen button on the keyboard just before or just after I place an order. Although I may not have the chance to save the image immediately, I will do so as soon as possible.

Next, as a position unfolds, I take note in my free-form journal of the things that first caught my eye about the trade and what led me to enter it where I did, as well as what my target and stop levels are and why. If I feel the urge to protect all or part of my position before these levels hit, then I will jot down the time and take another screen shot if possible. I will also try to express the reasoning behind this urge, even though I might end up ignoring it. I then follow the same process of capturing an image of my charts and writing down my reasoning when I finally close the position.

> Fleeting thoughts are just that, fleeting. So if you fail to write down your feelings while you are in a position, then you will have a more difficult time recollecting thoughts that crossed your mind as a position played out. It can be particularly difficult to remember the exact time within a position that different ideas came to you. Nevertheless, this knowledge is important when trying to apply lessons learned at those particular points in time to future trades.

Once you have a solid trading plan outlined, then your instincts become more finely honed through the process of applying that plan. The timing on your trades, however, can still be off and it might be difficult to discern which instincts are correct based upon your past experiences, and which ones are purely based upon fear or greed when things are not going according to plan as quickly as you may desire.

Analyzing your thought process as you make your way through the management of a position will help you gain a better sense of confidence in applying the techniques you worked out for a certain strategy before you trade them. It will also help you identify levels within those strategies that can cause difficulties and provide the opportunity for developing methods to deal with these levels. If you find that you still have a difficult time staying on track, then set aside certain periods throughout the day where you review your personal strategy guidelines. By keeping the strategies in the forefront of your memory, along with rules for trading them and the pros and cons that will apply, it is easier to stick to them when live opportunities present themselves.

## CHECK YOUR EMOTIONS

The reasoning behind your actions does not always have to be a question on the validity of your analysis. It could be more personal. If you are feeling ill and not quite yourself, whether it's a result of flu season, too much partying the night before, or insomnia, all of these can have a very visible impact upon how you perform in the markets. On the one hand, getting less sleep than usual can make some people follow their plans more closely and without as much of an emotional connection. On the other hand, grogginess can lead to some very costly mistakes.

Keeping a portion of your journal dedicated to how you are feeling from one day to the next, and the results of your performance on those particular days, can help you recognize when you are "in the zone," and when you should watch from the sidelines. I even go so far as to make a small note on the bottom of each of the charts I print out that describes how I felt that day and how confident I was in the position's success.

This step from the more passive, after-the-fact analysis to a more hands-on, knee-deep in the trenches, active analysis can be a tricky one to take. The more active you are, the more difficult it is to capture the data quickly enough to make notes on it. On the other hand, if you are not active enough, you can easily be paralyzed by over-analysis. It is easy to begin to second-guess your decisions and start to focus on watching the smaller time frames, since they will offer more visible action. The result is a tendency to try to read too much into every little support and resistance level that pops up, as well as every minor change in pace, instead of keeping an eye on the big picture. Whenever you find yourself faced with this tunnel vision, stop and walk away. Even if you only do so for a minute, at times this is all that is necessary to refocus upon your objectives.

## TONI'S TIPS

### Chapter 8

- My individual building blocks can represent different biases depending upon how each one combines with the other building blocks. This means that it is important to look for several things occurring together on a regular basis, such as declining volume on a gradual pullback in an uptrend into a support level at a correction period. These combined traits are core to a continuation buy setup, such as a bull flag.

- One of the easiest first steps to improving how you trade is to compile the charts from trades that you believe fall into the same category or type of setup. Put the winners in one pile and the losers in another. Next, select one of the building blocks to study how they impact the success or failure of your trades. Do most of the winners have similar qualities? How about the losing positions? If this is true, and yet the qualities between the winners and losers are different, then this can form the basis for improving your trade selection in that particular strategy. Use these observations to create lists of pros and cons for each building block on each type of setup you trade.

- Take the time to annotate your charts for your journal and point out specific traits that take place within the setup's development. For example, use a colored pencil to mark support and resistance levels if you print out your charts. It is beneficial to keep the colors you use consistent over time so that you can more quickly recognize patterns in the building blocks that make up a particular strategy.

- A large part of developing a successful trading strategy is willingness to make guesses. Some traits that initially appear positive may actually have very little impact upon the success of a setup, whereas other traits may seem relatively minor, but can actually impact the results of a position substantially. The more examples you compile, the clearer the overall picture will become.

- Capturing screen shots of your trades at critical points within their development, as well as jotting notes on what you are thinking throughout the management of a position can shed light upon whether it is logic guiding your instincts, or fear, and help you gain confidence in when to listen to the voices in your head and when to ignore them.

- Set aside certain periods throughout the day where you review your personal strategy guidelines. By keeping the strategies in the forefront of your memory, along with rules for trading them, and the pros and cons that will apply, it is easier to stick to them when live opportunities present themselves.

## A STEP FURTHER

Toni's style of market analysis and system development is based upon five core components of price development.

Describe Toni's Five Building Blocks of Price Development and their importance in understanding how price action unfolds.

_____

_____

_____

_____

_____

_____

_____

_____

_____

_____

_____

_____

_____

_____

_____

_____

For Toni's answer, go to www.traderslibrary.com/TLEcorner.

# 9

# ONLINE TRADING BLOGS

Trade logs and trade journals have been around for a long time. It is quite possible that the most well-known style of journaling in this day and age, however, is the online blog. Blogs are the evolutionary offspring of the online diary and the term itself is a contraction of the words "web log." The act of keeping a blog is called "blogging" and the author is referred to as a "blogger."

## BLOG BASICS

Blogs are believed to have their nascent beginnings in 1993, and gained a niche in 1999 before reaching the mainstream in 2004 as a popular political campaign tool. I landed in the unlikely realm of market education as an unintentional participant of this revolution. In the second half of the 1990s, a colleague and I created a website that documented our forays into the world of online trading almost from the moment I placed my first trade. It quickly gained a following and was picked up by one of the leading websites of the day that focused on educating traders. On it, I documented what stocks caught my interest and why. I attempted to explain the action I was seeing in those particular securities and how it might impact the future development of the price action in the stock I was interested in trading.

# BEGINNING YOUR OWN TRADING BLOG

Blogs come in many different styles and formats. Most are text-based and supplemented with other forms of communication, such as images, charts, videos, and links to other related blogs or websites of interest. They are typically displayed in reverse-chronological order with the most recent posts displayed at the top and older posts archived with what are referred to as "permalinks."

A number of sites exist that make keeping a blog very simple. You can select the style you wish or design your own. You do not have to know HTML codes or any other programming language to be able to maintain one, since you can easily write, upload images, or convert text to links all from the main menus or "create post" pages. You can type the word "blog" into any major search engine to locate the most popular blogging websites. Most of the sites that host blogs have easy-to-use search functions that will allow you to connect with other bloggers that share your interests.

## TAGGING

Before beginning any blog, there is one very important thing to consider: the usage of tags. Tags are keywords that you can attach to any of your blog posts. They are meant to inform you, as well as search engines and your general audience, what the main topics of your posts are. These are extremely handy for searching your blog for related topics, such as a particular type of setup, or even something you wrote in the past that you wish to compare to more recent activity.

The list of tags any blogger uses expands over time; however, I would highly recommend keeping a running list of the tags you use along the way to help keep them consistent. There are many words that you can use to describe certain traits, setups, types of securities, etc. Even slight variations can make it difficult to locate previous posts when desired. If you keep a core list, you can easily go back and insert links into a current post for your followers that reference similar activity or ideas from the past in addition to revisiting them yourself. It does not necessarily matter what you call something, but using terminology that is already popular in the field will help generate traffic and make you more affable to your fellow traders.

> Blogging offers a unique way to keep a trading journal since it is in the public forum. Although the majority of personal blogs are not widely followed, they can create a feeling of accountability that keeping a printed or hand-written journal does not offer. When you post a blog, the chances are high that someone else is going to read it. Over time, the blogs that are the most helpful to fellow traders will gain a devoted following.

Do not get too carried away though. Most blog platforms allow only a certain number of tags per post. If you discover that you are covering many topics in one entry, then divide it into smaller portions. This makes tagging easier, and it's more reader-friendly.

## HIGH-FREQUENCY POSTING

In order to maintain your following, you must post on a fairly regular basis. This can help keep some traders in line and prevent them from becoming too complacent regarding their efforts to excel through the use of a journal. It can also offer an outside source for fresh points of view, which can be very helpful. These can include anything from tips from other traders to questions that prompt you to visit a certain topic more thoroughly. The act of explaining your actions to others is quite rewarding, and I will explore this topic more in depth in Chapter 10.

# BLOGGING FOR TRADERS

A blog can be as simple or as complex as you wish. If time is on your side, then I would suggest including each of the following components:

- Trade examples and analysis
- Random musing or theories about your trading
- Your market view or outlook

Whenever you take the time to explain something, whether it's to another person or just for your own personal reference, you learn through that process. Time and time again I have touched upon this subject. It solidifies your thoughts, helps you build confidence in the truthfulness of those thoughts, and helps you identify flaws in your theories.

The best way to keep a trading blog is to write it with an audience in mind. Update it as if you were explaining what you are doing or thinking to a close friend sitting next to you. You may even wish to pretend that they don't know very much about the markets or trading, nor the strategies and methodologies you use, and that you are attempting to teach them this knowledge.

Be honest with yourself and your audience at all times. No one will expect you to be perfect. Don't beat yourself up over inaccurate conclusions. In fact, it is impossible to achieve 100% accuracy in this profession. Nevertheless, this is the one thing many traders never come to terms with. A blog is a way to step up and admit your struggles, as well as your triumphs, and to learn from them.

## WHAT GOES ON A TRADING BLOG?

The first component to consider including in your blog is screen shots of your trades and an analysis of the setups themselves. This can include the setups from a technical standpoint, as well as your thoughts on how you executed the trades, and what triggered these actions. When I am dealing with charts of my trades, I typically print out the charts and then mark them up manually with the things that catch my eye. For online posts, however, you will need to use an image editing program unless your charting platform has this function built in. If this is not available, then Microsoft Paint will suffice.

> Save the image of your annotated charts as .gif, .jpg, or .bmp files and then upload them to your blog using the upload image function on the blogging website.

When examining each trade you take, post each one as its own entry. I like to include the name I assigned to the particular strategy traded and the time frame I traded it on in the subject line of the blog entry. As with tags, this makes it easier to locate past entries when doing comparison studies.

Next, take a more in-depth look at your trade. Consider the following questions:

- How did I locate the trade?
- What is the primary time frame the trade took place on?
- What were the positive attributes of the position that attracted your interest?
- What were the potential cons?

When you are examining the pros and cons of the position, the simplest method is to list these traits while keeping my five building blocks of price action in mind, just as you would when keeping a loose-leaf journal. Create a heading for the pros of the position and then go through your list of building blocks, listing things under each category. Then repeat this for the cons.

## EXAMPLE BLOG POST

Figure 9.1 depicts a page from my journal of an after-hours trade that I took in the S&P 500 E-Mini futures. In my blog post, I have listed the pros and cons that caught my eye throughout the progress of this position. The strategy behind the trade was one that deals with advanced trend development techniques and combined the corrective waves of a typical trend. It was located by following a tick chart and the 15-minute and five-minute charts showing market data over all sessions. The entry, stop, and exit were determined using the one-tick chart.

Here is an example blog post based on that trade.

### 4th Wave Move, E-Mini S&P 500 (ES)

Immediately heading into this position, there were several factors that increased the risk. The most concerning was that the previous 2-wave correction had taken a lot longer to form than the one I traded had at that time I placed my entry. Knowing this, however, I kept my stop a little larger than average over the initial high labeled "I that took place heading into midnight. Once the second high was made within the congestion on April 14th, I moved my stop to two ticks above that second high.

When necessary, you will want to include notes on additional information such as this to explain your actions.

FIGURE 9.1: JOURNAL ENTRY - E-MINI S&P 500 (ES)

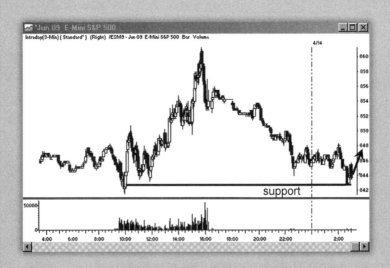

# Pros:

### Trend Development:

- The 3-wave trend completed itself and the channel broke, leaving room for a 4th and final flush (advanced trend analysis).

- A 2-wave correction developed off the lows from wave 3 on the downside.

### Support and Resistance:

- The upper end of support from previous day's congestion hit, but room remained for a stronger test of the support.

- The equal move support (a type of price support) left plenty of room for the ES to fall several points before the support would be too great to allow it to easily push further to the downside. This means the reward potential was greater than the risk.

### Pace:

- Wave 3 on the previous downtrend was the strongest wave of selling in the trend channel, creating higher odds for a slower correction and a better test of earlier support zone.

- The overall upside pace within the channel was slowing compared to downside pace.

- Once the range broke, the pace of the selling was stronger than the overall base.

### Volumes

- The range consisted of the lightest volume of the after-hours session despite support hitting, which suggested that bulls were still not convinced the downtrend was over.

- Once the range finally broke, volume increased somewhat to confirm the break.

### Correction Periods:

- The 2:00 am ET correction period became a pro after my entry.

# Cons:

### Trend Development:

- This form of 3-wave selling, a break in the downtrend channel, and a 4th wave of selling will typically be followed by a larger time frame reversal, but such a 4th wave is not always guaranteed, so there was a risk of a pace shift along the lower congestion that would not need another flush lower.

- At the time of my entry, the correction off the 3rd wave of selling was not quite as long as the previous two-wave correction that took place into 17:00 the previous afternoon, leaving room for a longer congestion. This ended up being the case.

### Support and Resistance:

- The previous day's congestion zone was already being tested, so it was uncertain how much more strongly it would attempt to do so.

### Pace:

- There was little to serve as a con immediately upon the early trigger, but the flush higher into 2:00 am ET created concern.

### Volume:

- Volume may have been light simply because that is the least active time for the markets.

### Correction Periods:

- No correction period to support my early entry.

When entering a trade such as the one of the ES, on a blog, the following tags would be useful for identifying additional trades with similar characteristics: bear flag, continuation, two-wave continuation, after-hours, pre-market, ES, equal move, 4th wave, and 2:00. I call this particular type of trend development a 4th wave move, so I have included this name in my tags. What this means is that the trend formed with three waves of downside, a longer base, and then a 4th wave that flushed out the trend prior to a larger reversal. After having seen specific trend development on numerous occasions, I gave it its own category that allowed me to study it more in depth.

Over time, you will also develop the skills to categorize variations of your own popular strategies. If you give them your own names, just be sure to include that name as a tag so that you can go back and compare different trades that fall into that same category.

## STYLE AND AUDIENCE

I wrote out each of the pros and cons in detail based upon the knowledge I have accumulated over the years. You can be more or less detailed if you wish. I wrote with an audience in mind that understands my basic style of analysis, but if you write to an audience of novices, then you will need to use greater detail to explain some of your reasoning for labeling each a pro or a con. This is because your reasoning is based upon experience, and your earlier studies show that each trait affects the outcome of that particular position—knowledge that your novice audience has not developed yet.

If you do wish to explain things on a more novice level, you can create permalinks that describe traits in detail, and then use shorthand references to this permalink when you post notes regarding a setup. This is not as easy, however, as having a reference section in your binder. Unless your followers keep another browser open or read your blog long enough to become familiar with your style, it can be difficult for them to follow along. If you do decide to go this route, then be sure to include a prominent link on your blog that discusses more of the details for your criteria so that new readers can quickly get up to speed.

# TRADE ANALYSIS ON YOUR BLOG

Other questions to consider when analyzing your trade are:

- What was your initial price target on the position, and why?

- Did the trade meet its objective, surpass its objective, or fail to hit it? If it surpassed your target or failed to hit your target, what could have contributed to this outcome?

- How confident did you feel when entering the setup?

- Was there any time while the position was open that you felt anxious? If so, make a note of when and try to identify what thoughts or feelings may have resulted in this state.

- Did you follow your plan from start to finish? If not, what impacted your decision to make a change?

- What lessons did you learn, or what rules or lessons were reinforced as a result of taking this trade?

# EXAMPLE TRADE ANALYSIS POST

In regard to the ES trade, my responses to each topic were as follows in this example of a trade analysis post.

**Target Reasoning:** Based upon an equal move and a stronger test of the previous support level.

**Trade Objective:** 843 Target zone – Exited several ticks above exact target. Target met.

**Confidence:** Wavered when ES flushed higher into 2:00. Concerned I would get pulled out before it had a chance to continue and would have to re-enter. Overall confidence of a better test of lows was strong.

**Anxious:** See above.

**Followed Plan:** Yes. Did not jump out early when ES flirted with stop level. Reminded myself that overall odds were strong and I could re-enter if necessary.

**Lessons Learned/Reinforced:** Stick to the plan. Do not bail early. Hold for Target zone as long as price development is still consistent with the pattern being created.

As you can see, there are a lot of things to consider when looking at each of your trades. Even if you are not an overly active trader, this task could easily take up several hours of your day. One option is to select the most noteworthy trades of the day, such as those you traded perfectly and those you completely messed up, and then detail these trades in your blog. This will reinforce your positive actions, while giving you a chance to look at your worst performers in more detail and potentially elicit feedback on them.

This same type of trade analysis can be applied to loose-leaf or freestyle forms of journaling as well, but keeping track of your trades in a blog is a bit different. It simply does not offer the analytical options of these other formats. Since posts are made chronologically, it can be more difficult to group similar topics or ideas together. The tags you use will be helpful, but it will not allow you to easily make side-by-side comparisons of your trades over time.

## TAKE IT ONE STEP AT A TIME

There is another option to consider regarding what trades you post and the information you include. Remember that one of the most important steps in keeping and analyzing any trading journal is to tackle only one problem at a time. Although you should still keep copies of the charts from all of your trades, as well as some basic notes on each, instead of uploading each of them to your blog, focus on just one topic at a time and devote a certain amount of time in your blog to just that topic.

For example, try posting only your trades that fall into the category of a trading range breakout for one to two months. Then focus solely upon the technical aspects of the trade and do not worry about the emotional component at first. I have done this in the past on message boards when other posters have challenged whether or not a setup can really be valid over time and offer enough opportunities to allow a trader to focus on trading just one setup. This is always a great way for a trader to refine their skills, although it can be easier to focus purely upon a single pattern when you are trading multiple stocks and securities as opposed to trading only one security. Otherwise, you may end up spending a lot more time sitting and waiting.

Questions to focus on for this type of trade analysis in your blog would be very similar to that of more detailed entries, but more precise for trade development:

- What is the primary time frame the trade takes place on?
- What were pros of the setup as they relate to Toni's five building blocks of price development?
- What were cons of the setup as they relate to Toni's five building blocks of price development?
- What was the target for the position and did it hit that target, exceed it, or fall short?

## REFLECTIONS

This type of analysis transitions smoothly into the second component to consider when keeping a trading blog: your reflections. Whether you choose to keep your theories in a hand-written journal, a word document, or on a blog, no journal can help you progress as quickly as one in which you take the time to study and reflect upon your trades.

Remember, guesswork is a key component of any journal. Use the tags you have created to keep track of other posts with similar observations and build a more comprehensive strategy. This will help add to your list of pros and cons on future trades and help you narrow down the instances in which you should press your edge versus those in which you should back off and either reduce your risk or wait for the next trade.

## FEEDBACK AND OTHER BENEFITS OF BLOGGING

Your random musings and theories may also attract the attention of your readers and invite them to participate in this thought process. They can offer their own interpretations for consideration and even guide you to other blogs whose style of trading is similar to your own or that may offer you tangible advice to incorporate into your system.

Many bloggers even earn a small stipend for their time by hosting advertisements that generate modest income from their traffic. Most will only earn enough to buy something from the local fast food joint at the end of the week, or a nicer dinner out at the end of the month, but I know of some that earn a decent enough return to fund regular vacations as a reward for their efforts. Some blog sites even exist that will pay you for posting on their sites.

# BLOGGING YOUR MARKET OUTLOOK

One of the best ways to build a following is to not only focus on your trades to date and your analysis built upon these, but also to include posts on your market outlook. This is the perfect opportunity to not only test out your skills as an analyst, but also help you build confidence in those skills. This market outlook is a step I take nearly every day. It serves as a guide for how I approach the markets that day because my analysis is based upon the larger time frames heading into each new trading session. Gauging the support and resistance levels, trend develpment, and pace of the price action in the indices gives me an edge in determining how passive or aggressive I should be and in which direction I should focus my greatest attention once the session is under way.

I try to read over my premarket analysis several times throughout the day, because I often find that my initial outlook is the correct one and that when I am going astray, it is because I am swaying from my original bias. There are a number of factors that can shift my bias once a session is under way, such as economic data or other news that can lead to price reversals or large gaps that can take out a lot of the potential I may have been expecting the evening before. Nevertheless, this remains an excellent starting point as well as another outlet for forging your skills.

Once you give an outlook on your blog, back it up with as many details as you can, but also list the potential cons. After the session has concluded, review your analysis and comment upon which aspects you felt had the greatest influence on the outcome of the market action. Also make a note of anything that shifted that bias intraday and led to a change in plans, or that might have caught you off guard.

As you explore other blogs, do not judge yourself by the progress of other bloggers that are posting their own results. Traders progress at their own speed and you cannot even be sure if others are being honest at times, since many people hate to admit their failures, even anonymously. New traders always ask me how long it will take before they will be earning a living from the markets. There is no definitive answer to this question.

The more you explore your own psyche and the more you learn from others' mistakes and triumphs, the shorter that learning curve will be. No matter what you may have been told, no one achieves long-term success in this field without bumps and bruises along the way, and two people attempting to apply the same methodologies can easily have dramatically different results.

# PROS AND CONS OF THE TRADING BLOG

I should warn you that maintaining an online trading blog can be very time-consuming—more so than another medium might be. It can also be very addictive, which would account for the "time-consuming" part! Since there is the presence of an audience, or at least the potential for one, it can enhance the feeling of responsibility. It is easier for many people to maintain a journal when they feel they are not just talking to themselves. This is perhaps why it is the primary form of a trading journal for many individuals.

What a blog does not offer is the ability to easily examine multiple facets of data and your trading history at once. I would not recommend using a blog in lieu of a trade log or loose-leaf journal. Instead, treat it as a supplement to these other methods and only do as much as time allows without letting it become all-consuming.

It is not necessary to include each of the three components I discussed. You may wish to begin with a blog dedicated to your market view and just take it from there. This is the core component of my own blog, which I then supplement with a variety of other types of entries as time allows. Alternately, you could select one setup that you trade and build a blog around learning to trade that particular setup. After a time, move onto something different.

Despite the potential drawbacks, the act of communicating to others (even a voiceless audience) can achieve insights not easily acquired elsewhere, and can make the act of keeping a trading journal more enjoyable and less like a required task. This makes it a format that every trader should at least consider. Some sites, such as www.stockticker.com, combine the aspects from all three styles of journals, from a trade log, to loose-leaf binder, to blog, into one platform. They can offer the advantage of being able to categorize your trades, run statistical analyses, observe your trades on multiple time frame charts, etc. You can even upload your trades directly from your brokerage platforms and then edit data such as stop placement and targets.

The multi-faceted characteristics of online journaling systems for trading can be quite appealing for data analysis. I still prefer to see all my charts splayed out in front of me, but this can be a much more efficient means of analysis for some individuals.

# TRADING SUCCESS TAKES TIME

No matter which style of journaling you wish to use, understand that short periods of success will not necessarily translate into a longer, nor equally successful, strategy or career. Take the time to really study and develop your strategies over time. While some systems will evolve that can be applied to all markets, these are typically quite in-depth. Looser-based systems will be more prone to falling in and out of favor at different phases in the market's overall trend. Learning to recognize when to press them, and when to back off and focus on other strategies, or just waiting out a less favorable period can take time. Additionally, your initial conclusions may be false and only apply to certain sets of circumstances, but not the pattern as a whole.

Recognizing what systems are based upon a run of luck versus those that will hold up over time is not a rapid process. Be patient. The goal is to develop a system that will keep you around for the long run. By using this style of analysis, however, you are on the right track and have a huge advantage over those that do not.

**TONI'S TIPS**

Chapter 9

- Keeping an online trading blog is one way to make your journal interactive, as well as provide a stronger motivation to maintain it over time.

- To make your blog searchable, use tags. These are keywords that list topics covered in a blog entry, and they can allow you and your viewers to more easily locate and compare a previous entry to current market activity.

- When you begin to keep a blog, there are three main categories that I would urge you to consider exploring, either one at a time or on an ongoing basis. These include trade examples and analysis, random musings or theories about your trading, and your overall market view or outlook.

- Throughout your blog, write with an audience in mind and approach it as if you were explaining your thoughts to a close friend.  Do not be afraid to admit your mistakes!

- Maintaining a blog can be very time consuming, and since entries are posted and organized chronologically, it can be more difficult to analyze over time. One option is to treat a blog as a supplement to other journaling methods and use it to address one topic at a time. For example, you might decide to spend several weeks exploring one specific pattern and the traits that create higher versus lower probability variations of that setup. Another topic would be to do a series of predictions on upcoming market behavior—attempt to explain why you believe that the current price action will result in the outcome you have propounded. Then review your predictions after the fact and attempt to explain any discrepancies. Once again, do not be afraid to guess!

- Online journaling programs can offer a trader many advantages over other journaling methods, and are worth considering. They can allow you to categorize your trades, run statistical analyses, observe your trades on multiple time frame charts, etc. Some will even allow you to upload your trade executions directly from your brokerage platforms and can be used to assist in stop placement and target projections.

**A STEP FURTHER**

There are a number of formats available to track your trades. Each has its strengths and weaknesses and some will offer greater appeal than others.

What are the main formats outlined in this book that are most commonly used as trading journals and what are their pros and cons?

_____

_____

_____

_____

_____

List some of your own strengths and weaknesses, and areas you would like to improve upon, and then use that list to consider which method of journaling would best suit you to begin with.

_____

_____

_____

_____

_____

For Toni's answers, go to www.traderslibrary.com/TLEcorner.

# PART 3

"The mediocre teacher tells. The good teacher explains. The superior teacher demonstrates. The great teacher inspires."

William A. Ward

# TAPPING INTO ADDITIONAL BRAIN POWER

Setting aside the time to reflect upon your journal entries is crucial to your development as a successful trader or investor. At times, however, it is beneficial to bring in another set of eyes, and not simply from the perspective of your online blog, but your core trade journal depicting all of your trades, as well. When you share your journal with others, it can provide a fresh light and a whole new way to look at things that you may not have even considered. To quote an old cliché, "Sometimes you don't even know what you have been missing until you find it."

## SEEING THINGS MORE CLEARLY

When I was in the fourth grade, I was having a lot of difficulty reading the chalkboard, and the strain on my eyes was causing headaches on nearly a daily basis. Unsurprisingly, when my parents took me in to have my eyes tested, it became obvious that I needed glasses. Although I certainly understood that this meant that my eyesight was not what it could be, I had no real understanding of just what this meant until I walked out the door of the clinic for the first time sporting my new pair of specs. I looked up at a tree and was amazed with what I saw. I stopped and just stared in awe at that tree for what seemed like an eternity. Although I was across the street, I could see the individual leaves as clearly defined as if they were right in front of me. It had never occurred to me that anything like this tree could be seen at a distance with such brilliant clarity.

I don't typically stop to wonder at the differences in being able to see with 20/20 eyesight versus what I have without my contacts or glasses anymore, but I am now keenly aware that such differences exist. Before that first trip to the optometrist, I did not understand the impact that less-than-perfect vision had upon my life. Glasses literally provided me with a new set of eyes, allowing me to look at the world from an enhanced point of view.

As a trader, you can't simply don a set of glasses to provide clarity to what you are working to achieve, but you can bring in another set of eyes. Enlist the help of someone that is already on the path to which you aspire. A lot of traders approach this quest by seeking out social networks and online communities such as message boards or chat rooms. These venues offer a place where they can interact with other traders in an effort to gain a better understanding of market dynamics, develop camaraderie with others, and bounce around ideas.

# INFORMATION OVERLOAD

A major drawback to this type of approach is that many of the individuals participating actively in these communities may not be any more successful than you are. Since at first it can be difficult to tell those who are and those who are not, they can actually hinder your development as a trader by causing you to try to go in too many directions at once. "You have to use this indicator!"; "No, that one doesn't work well, but this system is unbeatable!" With so many websites and self-proclaimed market gurus out there, it is overwhelming to try to discern which direction to follow. Unfortunately, while a number of them are reputable and can provide valuable lessons, the vast majority are simply out for a quick buck, and many go no further than to rehash material you can find for free by doing a basic internet search.

# WORDS FROM THE WISE

We all know that "making it" in this profession is difficult. It takes a great deal of hard work and a lot of determination. There are shortcuts, however, if you know where to look and are lucky enough to find those willing to help guide you along the way. One of the most successful shortcuts is enlisting the help of a mentor or coach. Very few individuals make it to the top of any field without one.

## MENTORS

In Homer's *The Odyssey*, Mentor, also known as Mentes, was Odysseus' trusted elderly counselor. When Odysseus left for the Trojan War, he placed Mentor in charge of the care of his son Telemachus. While he was away, the goddess Athena, who was the Greek goddess of wisdom, often disguised herself as Mentor to guide and counsel Telemachus. Today, the word "mentor" is defined as "a trusted counselor or guide."[1]

Throughout history, the relationship between a mentor and his protégé, more commonly referred to these days as "mentee," can be cited as a major contributor to the development of talent. For instance, Aristotle served as a mentor to Alexander the Great, Johann Christian Bach to Wolfgang Amadeus Mozart, and more recently, Martin Scorsese to Oliver Stone.

## THE BEGINNING OF THE JOURNEY – FINDING WHAT ATTRACTS YOU

I entered the markets with a certain degree of understanding about the relationship between a mentor and a mentee, although I had never fully embraced it. I had come from a strong background in the arts, but was often at odds with what popular culture was dictating as aesthetically pleasing at the time. As a realist, my appreciation for the world of abstract art was quite narrow, and I'm afraid I must admit this to be true to this day. However, nearly every major painter in history was once a student or apprentice to a master artist that had already been practicing their art for a living. Those that studied under them drew upon that wealth of knowledge, even when over time, their own personal style may have developed into another approach to painting altogether.

---

1    Merriam-Webster's Collegiate Dictionary, 11th Edition

From the moment I first expressed an interest in the financial markets, a number of books on the topics of trading and investing were foisted upon me. Unfortunately, technical analysis was still seen as a fringe science in many circles. The focus was more upon longer-term fundamental analysis as opposed to anything dealing with the nascent arena of online trading, and particularly the forms of trading known as day trading or swing trading. For me, the vast majority of these fundamental analysis texts were the theoretical equivalent of abstract paintings. While the underlying meaning may be apparent to some, to me it looked like a Jackson Pollock piece.

Now, before I incite a riot, I do feel that fundamental analysis does have its place, as does Pollock. However, while I can appreciate that such proponents of these styles exist and derive a great deal of value from their points of view, it simply does not attract me. What did attract me was the field of technical analysis. Instead of taking pieces of various financial reports and putting them together to try to create a picture, I prefer looking at charts depicting price and volume activity. To me, these are akin to viewing a digital snapshot of a particular security. The picture itself is instantly available and the data it displays up until that point in time is indisputable, although as in the case of any piece of art, the meaning behind it is still up for interpretation.

## FINDING THE RIGHT MENTOR

Given my attachment to the technical aspects of price development, finding a mentor was not an easy task and not one I was comfortable pursuing. At the time, most of the successful technical analysts I met had come from the trading pits and had the bravado, swagger, and "men's locker room" mentality to attest to it. This was like night to day for someone who grew up in a small town in the middle of the American heartland. Being a female in a male-dominated industry did not help either, since role models of the same gender were extremely few and far between, and virtually untouchable from my point of view as a "mere mortal."

Although I did have a small group of acquaintances that I kicked around trading ideas with, for the most part, I took the path of becoming my own mentor. I used the skills that I had developed as a student as well as an artist and began to diligently study the market from the point of view of a chartist. I began to integrate the use of a journal into my trading. My knack for pattern recognition quickly helped me excel, first as an analyst and then as a trader, as I developed confidence in my analytical abilities. This journey, however, took many years.

## A NETWORK OF TRADERS

These days I am lucky enough to have found a strong circle of professional traders with whom I can share my ideas and learn from as well. No matter how much you think you know or understand about the market, there is always more to learn than you would have ever conceived. To this day, I still pick up tricks and insights from my fellow traders that I borrow, adapt, and then apply to my own style of analysis and trading. A number of breakthroughs in my own trading may never have happened, or may have taken quite a bit longer to have happened, without that interaction.

# A GUIDE THROUGH TRADING TRAPS

Although it is certainly possible to become successful without a mentor, having one can help you avoid a lot of unnecessary pain and frustration along the way. It will undoubtedly save you a great deal of energy, time, and money. While it is fun, unless you have the proper guidance right from the beginning, trading can also be quite expensive. Many of the most costly mistakes are easily avoided.

We have all heard basic words of so-called financial wisdom, such as "Always keep your stop," or "Never average down," or "The trend is your friend." What a mentor can teach you, however, are the circumstances in which each and every one of these sage words can prove false.

For instance, stop levels on a position you have bought are often support levels. If the momentum of a sell-off into the support zone is slowing, then the zone itself can still hold and once again reverse higher, even though the exact price of your earlier-set stop may hit. A mentor can teach you how to recognize when this is likely to be the case and help you still maintain adequate risk parameters so that you avoid "blowing a stop" simply because you did not keep your exact stop. At the same time, you are able to maintain a position in a security that still has a high probability of bouncing sharply higher, albeit off a slightly lower low.

When you get a chance to speak with any trader who is more experienced than yourself, you are opening yourself up to the potential for greater personal development. Those who have "come before you" typically have a firmer understanding of the nuances of market activity than you do. They can also understand the financial and emotional roadblocks that stand in your way, because they had to overcome many of them as well. Their knowledge can help you avoid falling into some of the common traps or pitfalls they have experienced, or have seen happen to their colleagues, and they can also share with you some of their own tips, tricks, and solutions to problems that you may also be experiencing.

How often have you found yourself frustrated because your stop or trailing stop on a position hits just before a huge move takes place, like I mentioned? It could be that you also simply need some assistance understanding how to place stops correctly and adjust them so that this does not happen as often. More experienced traders are a great place to seek out such advice!

## RECOGNIZING TROUBLE SPOTS

Your journals will paint the picture of both your strong suits and those areas where you struggle. Stop placement problems, for instance, are some of the easiest things to correct based upon a study of the trades in your journal. As a novice trader, it might take a few years to really understand the patterns in your trading and work out adequate measures to avoid many of the errors you have been unknowingly making.

To someone who has a greater understanding of price action, however, your mistakes may be recognizable within just a couple of minutes of flipping through the charts depicting your executions. Think of how much money, time and frustration such could be saved with some assistance in this area! True, you may be able to reach the same conclusions yourself over time, just as I did in this particular area, but I would much rather have been able to take a short cut!

# NO ONE KNOWS EVERYTHING

Theoretically, everyone can benefit from having a mentor. In reality, however, the mentor/mentee relationship can be rather complex and does not work for everyone. Enlisting the assistance of another individual requires a person to first and foremost admit that she does not, in fact, know it all—and that she could actually benefit from the knowledge of others.

Stop and think for a minute about your own personality, as well as the personalities of those who are closest to you. Are you the type of person that will stubbornly keep at a task no matter how frustrated you become, are you someone that will seek assistance right away, or do you fall somewhere in between? We all have weaknesses, but people approach their personal weaknesses in different ways. Some will appear to accept them and move on, without attempting to find a way to better themselves in the process, whereas others will seek to understand their weaknesses and work to find ways to improve how they approach and deal with these weaknesses.

# LEARN TO LET GO

Let's say that you are trying to open a jar of pickles, and no matter how tightly you grip the jar in one hand and the lid in the other and twist, you simply cannot get the lid to budge. What lengths will you go to in order to open that jar, assuming that your desire to obtain a pickle is all that you can think about at the moment? I know quite a few people who would keep attempting to twist the lid off by hand and become increasingly more irritated by the effort before finally either giving up and settling on some other less desirable snack, or asking someone else for help. Typically that help would entail merely handing the jar to someone else to open. If this sounds like you, you may not be ready for a mentor.

# TAKE RESPONSIBILITY FOR YOUR TRADING EDUCATION

In order for a mentor-mentee relationship to work, you must not only admit that your methods could benefit from the knowledge of another approach, but you also must be willing to put in the effort to apply the knowledge you acquire. A mentor cannot do the work for you. He is there to serve as your navigator, to provide you with insight that can lead to another way to approach a given problem, or to enhance already favorable qualities in your trading. He is not there to remove the lid from the jar himself.

He is there to show you some of the tricks you can use to open the jar yourself, many of which may have never even crossed your mind. He can also inspire you to create your own methods to remove the lid and encourage your train of thought, guiding you back on track when you begin to lean towards the impractical or absurd, and showing you how your mindset on what *qualifies* as the impractical or absurd may need to be altered.

I know at least half a dozen tried-and-true methods to easily remove even the most stubborn lid on any jar. One of the most unconventional involves the use of two shoes, but if you did not read this particular paragraph in this particular book, how likely would you have been to have even considered using your shoes to remove the lid of a jar? Even upon reading this paragraph, are you able to make the connection and figure out how it is done? If you find yourself quite curious as to just what the "half a dozen" methods are that I employ in such a task, and are still trying to figure out how shoes come into play, you may be ready for a mentor after all!

## SEARCHING FOR INSPIRATION

For most of us, the people who we look up to and from whom we draw our inspiration may not always be in our same field of interest. Nevertheless, taking the time to seek out and get to know others that have already accomplished some of the goals you have set for yourself is one of the best ways to reach your own goals more quickly. As traders, we may gain inspiration from many venues, but no one can really understand the mindset of a trader like another trader.

The difference is not unlike that of watching a war being documented in the news and offering advice based upon what you have learned in your history books and the autobiographies of veterans versus actually being in the midst of the fighting and the struggle to survive. Failing to survive in the markets may not have mortal consequences for most, but the risks of financial and/or emotional devastation are quite real. If you intend to survive, you better have a very strong plan in play to begin with and develop the ability to learn and adapt quickly. By taking the time to reflect upon your journal entries, you are already honing that ability. Bringing in another point of view will help shed even more light upon your progress.

The spectrum of types of traders is very wide, and while you may find others with styles similar to your own, you will not likely find two traders who approach the markets in an identical fashion. This can make the attempt to find a mentor in this industry highly frustrating, but it can also be a great advantage. Finding those whose style you feel compliments your own methodologies takes time. Searches on the internet yield so many results these days that it is virtually impossible to sort out the professionals from the rest of the bunch. In reality, many of the professionals don't even have the time to keep up an active internet persona. We are too busy following the market. Even though I've been in the public eye myself for over a decade, this is something I have struggled with immensely. Just ask my publisher who laments that, even at 4:00 in the morning, I am trading instead of writing!

Do not lose hope too quickly though. While it is true that many professional traders will not have the time to interact with you on a personal basis, social networking and trading clubs around the world now offer traders a chance to communicate on a scale never before dreamed possible. Message boards, online trading expos, and clubs were all in their infancy when I first entered the markets. Now, traders throughout the world are sharing their experiences each and every day, not only on message boards, but also on blogs, online video sharing websites, personal home pages, and much more.

Yes, it can still take time to find like-minded individuals, but the bonus in today's information age is that once you find one or two people whose methodologies catch your eye, you can check out those with whom they associate and have an instant network of other traders whose styles are also similar. This is accomplished by following their web links, checking out the profiles of their friends, joining their chat room, stopping by their local trading club meeting, etc. Some of those you come across are bound to be the social types who love to share and interact with others, bouncing ideas back and forth. Approximately half the traders that frequent my own chat room have been active in the markets full-time since at least the late '90s.

Another way to seek out experienced traders that is once again gaining in popularity is to join one of the small trading floors or private equity management groups that can be found throughout the country. Essentially, these are offices that contain a number of individual trading desks that allow traders to have the experience of "going into the office," as opposed to trading from home. These can be set up in many ways, but since the costs of trading with one of these venues are typically much less than most individual traders can receive on their own, and most offer much greater leverage as well, many professional traders will trade through them. Some firms will also offer access to research and educational tools at these locations that is difficult to receive elsewhere.

# BE AGGRESSIVE

In order to locate a mentor, you have to be somewhat aggressive in nature. Most people you meet online, or even in passing at a firm set up with live trading desks are not going to offer anything more than a few tired clichés until they get to know you well, such as, "Don't put all your eggs in one basket." If you drop by a trading chat room, they are likely to be more focused upon what is going on in the market at the moment or just shooting the breeze than they are in taking the hand of someone with less experience who wishes to learn from their expertise.

You may think that you are ready to seek out a mentor, but do you have the gumption to put your neck out on the line at the risk of seeming impertinent? Additionally, do you know where to draw the line once you have stuck your neck out? If you do not ask enough questions, or do not ask the correct ones, you will learn very little and not easily catch the attention of someone who might otherwise be willing to take you under their wing. If you ask too many questions or pose them inappropriately, you may come across as obnoxious or disrespectful, and those who may have been willing to share will keep quiet for fear that you will prove to be a distraction. Have patience. Don't be afraid to "lurk" in a room of experienced traders. Over time, your mere presence will show your desire and sincerity, and you will start to develop an understanding of how others in that forum succeed, as well as learn some of the major pitfalls of those who don't.

# THE COACH VERSUS THE MENTOR

Initially, you may find it too difficult to find a mentor through the means I have discussed thus far. Or, you may find that, while you have learned a great deal from such interactions, you have yet to find people that will take enough of their own time to really examine where you are coming from as a trader and offer you advice tailored specifically to your own personality and individual strengths and weaknesses. To receive such individual attention, you may find that a coach is necessary. A *coach* in this sense is merely a mentor who charges for their time, and therefore has a more vested interest in your success.

As a professional trader, I am bombarded every day with questions regarding my opinion on one topic or another, such as requests by individuals to look at this strategy or that, and offer ways in which I think they may be improved. Years ago it was fairly easy for me to find the time to do this and I worked with hundreds of traders, offering assistance for free. This was long before kids and other obligations began to place additional demands upon my time.

As any single parent can attest to, attending to the needs of your kids alone takes up to six hours of each weekday, between assisting with homework, making dinner, overseeing chores, and just spending time together as a family. In the past, this was time that I would spend communicating with other traders, but these days two little people in particular take precedence and limit the time I have available to work with traders on an individual basis. As a result, I have moved in the direction of coaching and teaching other traders on a larger scale.

# TRADING TAKES TRAINING

It has been my experience that a coach is a hybrid mentor. A good comparison between a regular mentor and a coach can be made by stopping by a local gym. When you join a gym for the first time, you are going to cross paths with a number of individuals who are much more dedicated to the maintenance of their physique than you have been up until that point. If you strike up some friendly conversation, you are likely to learn a number of tips for achieving a level of fitness similar to their own. Over time, once you begin to show real progress, they may even join you in a workout or two. They will not, however, make it their goal from the moment they meet you to push you to attain their same level of fitness. If you want that type of interaction, you are typically going to have to hire a personal trainer.

This brings us to a somewhat interesting and even controversial topic. How does a person find a trading coach, and is it worth paying for one? Finding a good trading coach can be a great deal more difficult than finding a good personal fitness trainer, and the latter is difficult enough as it is. Not only must you have a good idea of what style of trading you wish to learn in order to first find a coach, but establishing their credentials can be disconcerting at times.

## WHAT IS IT WORTH?

If you want the best, you often must be prepared to pay top dollar, but paying top dollar in this industry does not necessarily ensure that you receive the best coaching, only the best marketing team. These days, many offer so-called track records of their performance, but time has taught me that these are virtually worthless. Not only are many done with methods that might be compared to the questionable accounting methods and financial statements from many corporations involved in the 2008 global financial meltdown, but merely having a good trading record in no way qualifies a person to actually impart their knowledge successfully to others. Nor does it mean that their methods would even work well with the other trader's own personality. Many traders who also offer education, like myself, will freely share some of their knowledge in the format of magazine articles, free webinars, speaking engagements, etc. This gives readers the opportunity to discover whether or not their styles and personalities may be a decent fit. In the end, the only way to really tell whether they can assist you or not is to book a session and try for yourself.

When interviewing a coach, it is very important to keep in mind that you are looking for someone to still serve as a mentor. While you can learn techniques through courses and seminars, it can take a bit of time to discern which techniques are best suited to your personality. It then takes longer to learn where you are struggling to apply these techniques, as well as the areas in which you excel. Your trading journal will be an integral part of the relationship you will have with your coach.

Just as any personal trainer worth their muster will have you track your food intake, exercise, performance levels, etc., a coach who is dedicated to taking your trading to the next level will also need to closely monitor your performance. In order for this relationship to succeed, you must be dedicated to providing them with the information they need to judge and monitor your progress. If you make this effort, then a coach is well worth it. You can often pay for a session with your coach in a single trade by identifying just one bad habit and learning how to recognize it in time to avoid it in the future.

A good coach or mentor will help you focus your thoughts and make sense out of your actions, allowing you to develop as an individual and not as a clone. She will share with you the knowledge that she has acquired over the years and offer you insights into how you can adapt that knowledge to fit your own style. Through this process, she can show you what worked for her, as well as what didn't. She can even share with you how others she has worked with or whom she is friends with have dealt with the same types of weaknesses you may be working to overcome, even if she has not experienced them first-hand.

If you study and reflect upon your journal regularly, the chances are that you will be able to work through many issues on your own and progress at a decent pace, but this process can easily take months if you are an experienced trader, and years if you are a complete novice.

## TEACHERS MAKE THE BEST STUDENTS

To take the concept of mentoring a step further, I cannot understate the importance of "passing it on." As I stated earlier in this section, I have been working with other traders since the mid '90s, sharing with them what I have learned over the years and helping them to make sense out of their own trading. I can honestly say, had I not taken up the role of mentor rather early on in my trading career, I would not still be trading today.

As I mentioned earlier, my very first trading journals were not kept in a notebook, but rather on a website in a form that was unconventional at the time, but would be most akin to a blog by today's standards. On this website, I shared which stocks I was looking at and what attracted me to them. I would then detail the results of my trades, seeking to explain why I set my entry and stop levels where I did, how I placed my targets, how I managed the positions, etc. By forcing myself to spell out in detail each and every action I made, I created a record that could then be studied and analyzed over time. This practice allowed me to map out strategies and offered proof for the results of actions that would otherwise have just been labeled intuitive or instinctive, without understanding which instincts were based upon emotional responses and which were based upon logic.

When I took this practice a step further, calling my trades live in a chat room, it forced me to be even more careful that my assertions were true to the best of my knowledge. Eventually, I began to work one-on-one with traders on their individual trading. By doing so, it offered a fresh look into strategies and concepts that I had simply not focused on in the past. It also showed me how others were approaching patterns that I was already using, but managing differently.

By this time I had already developed a system of market analysis that could be applied to any type of price action by breaking it down into core components. I would take this system of analysis and apply it to the strategies my clients were using, showing them how to avoid their most common mistakes, as well as to create checklists and templates for the styles of setups they were most drawn to already. Naturally, this approach has expanded my own repertoire of strategies over time, and has helped me gain a firmer understanding of different types of price development that I may have had no interest in previously.

Working with less experienced traders, or those that come from a different trading or investing background than yourself, who are interested in having you share your style with them, also helps you build confidence in the knowledge that you already possess. It should also strengthen confidence in your ability to diminish many of the emotional hurdles most traders are faced with. One of the biggest hurdles that many traders have is developing a strategy that they feel is sound, but then struggling to implement that strategy. They constantly question whether or not they have made the correct assumption when they locate a setup they believe fits their criteria. They hesitate at the exact moment that they should be executing the trade. This hesitation, resulting from what essentially amounts to a lack of confidence in their system, can result in missed opportunities or sub-par setups.

When day trading or scalping, you often have only seconds to execute a trade correctly. If you hesitate, then you miss the best entry or exit price for your position. On the other hand, if you hesitate—going back and forth on your decision before finally taking a trade—and the security has not started moving favorably during what should be those key moments, this could be a sign of weakness for that particular trade, and the extra time you had to enter the trade is really a con. Instead of being a gift, it can sometimes increase the odds that the setup will fail. It could also mean that you entered too early and will then have to wait for more corrective action, thus giving you time to doubt your analysis and execution. This can cause a trader to get jumpy and bail before giving the trade a chance to work out.

When you share your knowledge with others, it invites them to question your assertions. You have to explain why your rules are what they are and what led you to make those rules in the first place. This vocalization of your beliefs helps internalize them, which ultimately leads to less hesitation when you see the setups that you have taught to others beginning to develop within a security. The process of proving your concepts to be viable also allows you to locate flaws in your system and adjust. Teaching others what you know can even help you develop new setups or strategies that build upon or result from the follow-through of the setups you were originally focused upon teaching.

# PARTNERSHIP

In many ways, the relationship between a mentor and a mentee or a coach and a client becomes a partnership in which both sides benefit. They both progress and grow as traders or investors at a pace that would be difficult to replicate if either person were moving forward on their own. While it may take a little time to find a good fit, the knowledge and confidence gained from such an endeavor can be more than worth the effort it takes to do so.

By enlisting the aid of a mentor or coach, or serving as one, it doesn't take long before most traders start to come across many of those "things they never knew they were missing!"

# TONI'S TIPS

## Chapter 10

- As traders, we never stop learning from our experiences. However, if you enlist the advice of others who can take on the role of mentors, it will accelerate your learning curve. They can share with you their tricks and insights into trading and the markets, help you avoid mistakes they have made or have seen numerous others make along the way, and offer feedback on your trading journal that can result in immediate improvement in your trading and investing skills.

- Before enlisting the help of a trading coach, realize that a worthwhile coach will require you to actively participate in your education and is not there to just give you lessons. Just like a personal fitness trainer will have you keep a record of what you are eating and the activities you are participating in on a day-to-day basis so that he can help tailor your meal and exercise plans and tweak them when necessary, a trading coach will need to be able to study and analyze your trades and the steps you have been taking to push ahead in the markets. Keeping a proper trading journal is an absolute necessity. It allows the coach to gain a firm understanding of the level you are at and what your strengths and weaknesses are, so that he can focus upon areas that will offer you the greatest benefit from the beginning.

- Share the knowledge you acquire along the way with other traders. By putting your thoughts into words, you can quickly build confidence in your own beliefs. This can also help you identify areas in your strategies that need greater clarification or should be explored in further detail. The feeling you receive when someone thanks you for helping them succeed doesn't hurt either!

## A STEP FURTHER

The learning curve in trading is quite intense. It takes most traders a great deal longer than anticipated to see the rewards they desire. This curve can be decreased dramatically when you tap into the knowledge of more experienced traders, or even those with a somewhat different style of trading. They will often see things in your own trades that you may not recognize and can offer insights and guidance that will save you a great deal of both time and money. Even the mere act of sharing your own knowledge with others will reinforce your rules in your own mind. Consider the options laid out in this chapter as potential reserves of knowledge that can assist you in your quest and be sure to carefully weigh the pros and cons of each.

What kind of mentor relationship offers the greatest appeal to you and why?

_____

_____

_____

_____

_____

_____

_____

_____

_____

What steps do you need to take to integrate one or more of these types of relationships into your life?

_____

_____

_____

_____

_____

_____

_____

_____

_____

_____

For Toni's answer, go to www.traderslibrary.com/TLEcorner.

# PART 4

"We are what we repeatedly do. Excellence, then, is not an act, but a habit."

Aristotle

# CULTIVATING THE MINDSET OF A PROFESSIONAL TRADER

Knowing why it is beneficial to maintain a trading journal that documents your exploits and progress in the financial arena, and knowing how to create the type of journal that aids in this field of personal development are merely two components necessary to ensure your success in the markets. In addition, you must also possess the willpower to put that knowledge to use and make it part of your daily and weekly routine.

## RESISTANCE TO CHANGE

As human beings, we have the tendency to resist change. We each have our own comfort zones and at times it can be difficult to push ourselves to really commit to something new, even when logic tells us that it is necessary to implement change in order to attain our goals. If you are like most people, you have made a number of resolutions to make changes in your life, and yet one month after having resolved to reach a goal, you find yourself no-where close to where you had intended to be by that time.

## CULTIVATING A GOAL

New Years' Day is always a favorite time for new intentions to be seeded. The problem is that merely sticking a seed in the ground does not guarantee that it will germinate and grow to reach its full potential. That seed must first have been planted in fertile soil. It must then be nurtured, by man or by the benefits of its native en-vironment, overcoming many obstacles along the way. If it receives too much water or too much sun, it may perish. If it does not re-ceive enough, it may perish. It must also withstand unexpected changes in the weather and survive the onslaught of pests and dis-ease in order to flourish.

When a seed is tossed about and carried by the wind, the chances that it will land in an ideal locale and develop into a mature plant are very slim. I will be the first to admit that even with my good intentions, many of the seeds I have planted ended up failing. Even as I look out into my courtyard now, I see reminders of those fail-ures. My tomato plant has succumbed to some sort of blight, with each of its flowers turning brown and falling off before they can turn into tomatoes. My fern is a rather ill shade of yellow. My son's marigold, which he planted last spring, has surprised us all with its resilience, although the flowers it has produced are a mere shadow of the ones I recall from my mother's own garden.

Does the fact that my courtyard is essentially a failure mean that I do not have a "green thumb," or that I am destined to kill, or severely maim, or cause damage to anything and everything I decide to plant? No, of course not. It does, however, mean that I will need to put in a much greater effort than I am presently if I wish for my initial intentions to actually succeed. As those who have attempted to grow anything from seeds already know, the chance that any individual seed has to fully mature improves substantially when its environment is carefully monitored and controlled.

Anyone can learn how to grow a certain type of plant. Simply go to the library, or, better yet, visit a local nursery that specializes in the particular plant you wish to cultivate. Learn about the obstacles you potentially face, such as the types of diseases or insects most likely to prey upon your plant and how to guard against such threats. Most of us will have the actual ability necessary to carry this out. Taking the time to apply the knowledge learned in these books and from these authorities is somewhat simple. It is carefully monitoring and caring for the plant to the point that it becomes a habit, rather than a chore, where most of us fail.

In this chapter, we will be examining what it takes to turn the act of keeping a trading journal into a habit, pushing past the tendency to resist change, in order to cultivate a successful career in the markets

> Consult those who are renowned as authorities on the subject matter at hand and be prepared for the potential obstacles that may come your way.

# STICK-TO-IT-TIVENESS

One of my all-time favorite quotes, and one that I have taped to the wall above my main monitor as a constant reminder, is from B.C. Forbes, the well-known author and founder of *Forbes* magazine. Mr. Forbes stated that, "No man can fight his way to the top and stay at the top without exercising the fullest measure of grit, courage, determination, resolution. Every man who gets anywhere does so because he has first firmly resolved to progress in the world and then has enough stick-to-it-tiveness to transform his resolution into reality.…" This "stick-to-it-tiveness," as Forbes calls it, is quite often the only difference between those who succeed at a task versus those who fail. Knowing why you should do something and knowing how to do something, whether it's keeping a trading journal or losing 50 pounds, mean very little if you are not fully resolved to take that knowledge and act upon it. Not only must you act upon it, you must also make it a habit. In other words, you must *stick to it*!

At the beginning of one summer I had a vision. In it I pictured large, ripe, red, juicy tomatoes. I decided to act upon this vision and planted a few tomato seeds in fertile soil, thanks to the potting mixture purchased at a local home improvement center. When my seeds sprouted and began to grow, I selected the two largest plants and moved them into big clay pots. I placed them in a nice, sunny location, and watered them regularly. I took very good care of my tomato plants at first. When it became obvious the branches needed support, I added a wire support system so that they would not fall under the weight of the tomatoes and break off. I even built them a stand to make them less accessible when my cat decided that the leaves of a tomato plant were quite tasty.

As the summer wore on, however, I grew frustrated at how small my tomatoes were and how long it took for the new tomatoes to ripen. Soon I became less diligent. I would forget to water my tomato plants, and they would often wilt sadly in the sun. Then they began to develop little spots on the leaves. I was uncertain of what was wrong and how to remedy the situation. Instead of trying to figure out how to correct the problem, I did nothing. As the plants continued to deteriorate, I concluded that the cost in terms of both the time and money necessary to correct the problems befalling my haphazard garden outweighed any potential reward I would gain from taking the actions necessary to succeed in this particular venture.

The fact that I gave up on my gardening attempt that summer had very little impact on my present and future lifestyle. It merely created a slight inconvenience. Instead of being able to walk out my door and pick what I needed for my salad or pasta dish, I had to rely on tomatoes purchased at the store or local farmers' market. These were already frequent stops, so even the inconvenience factor was virtually nonexistent.

Consider for a moment, however, how this same mindset, which tells us "not to bother" to undertake one task or another, can affect other areas of our lives. What happens when the consequences of inaction are greater than not being able to pick a tomato when you want it? Perhaps your resolution involves losing weight, exercising more regularly, or quitting smoking? The consequences of neglecting to take care of our own health are certainly greater than taking care of the health of a tomato plant. The rewards of doing so, however, are also greater. And yet, more often than not, relatively few people achieve these long-term goals as compared to those who had "resolved" to do so last January 1st.

When many individuals first resolve to become a trader or to manage their own investment portfolio, they are often throwing seeds into the wind. Some individuals that embark upon this path will get lucky enough to land in the right positions and be profitable right away, but merely landing in the right place is only part of the picture. Some of the seeds will germinate and begin to grow where they land, but most will wither and die by some means or another. Typically the only thing that allows an individual long-lasting success when they are initially favored by chance or luck is that they land in an environment that has allowed their seed, or seed money, in this case, to grow strong enough, and that they are given enough time to learn how to combat the elements working against their success.

Others realize early on that, to succeed, it takes more of an effort than simply sowing a thought into their head, opening an account, and buying or selling whatever security suits their whim. Those that take their desire to succeed a step further are like our would-be horticulturalists. They take the time to go to the library and nursery. They make the effort to seek out authorities who could help improve their chances of growing a fully mature, hearty plant or garden. They invested in the fertilizer and recognized the need to provide some care for their venture, so-to-speak.

# TAKE IT A STEP FURTHER

Even with a certain degree of education, however, most traders are still not able to reach their goals. They may have acquired enough knowledge that they should theoretically be able to be successful, but they do not know how to take what they have learned, develop a system from that knowledge, and tailor it to their own personality; hence giving them that extra edge of a true professional.

How does a person take that final step? Perhaps they already learned this lesson in another area of their life, or maybe a colleague steered them in the right direction. Then again, maybe they just happened upon this book in a local bookstore and it caught their eye. No matter how they got there, at some point they came to the realization that systematically recording, reviewing, and reflecting upon their activities in the market, as well as their emotional and personal life as it relates to the market, will put them on a completely different level from the masses and give them the best chance to reach their goals.

# APPLYING DISCIPLINE

Acting upon knowledge requires discipline. The term "discipline" can be defined as "control gained by enforcing obedience or order."[2] Given that you are still reading this book, obviously one of your goals at this point is to learn how you can take the knowledge from this book and use it to create and maintain a

---

2     Merriam-Webster Collegiate Dictionary, 11th Edition

trading journal of your own. It is relatively easy to begin keeping a journal. You have probably already printed out charts of your most recent trades or investments.

In order for an act to become a habit, however, a person must apply discipline. The "stick-to-it-tiveness" that Forbes remarked upon is merely another way to say that you must be disciplined in both your actions and your resolve in order to reach a goal. At first, it will take an effort on your part to maintain this discipline, but over time, your actions become a habit and will require less and less of an "obvious" effort.

## DISCIPLINE, PROFESSIONALISM, AND LIFE

When applying discipline to the creation and maintenance of a trading journal, it can be extremely useful to think of journaling as a job requirement. Your goal is to become a professional trader, or, at the very least, to be able to trade and invest at the skill level of a professional. As such, participation in the market at any level should be taken with the same level of seriousness you would apply to any job you might undertake at a professional level. Your desire should be akin to the gardening enthusiasts who have achieved a flawless reputation, and hence top dollar, for their produce. They attained that level of success by carefully monitoring and adjusting the amount of light, water, and additional care necessary for their plants to flourish. If they intend to have record crops year after year, you can bet that they keep excellent records of what they have done to lead them to their current level of success. You can accomplish the same thing in the financial markets by employing the same techniques. In other words, take the act of maintaining a trading journal seriously!

People who have discipline in other areas of their life are going to have an easier time staying on the right path with their journal. I've done a lot of one-on-one personal mentoring and coaching with traders over the years, and a journal is something that I require from each of them. Some of them take to it and stick to it immediately, while others seem to avoid it like the plague!

Often, it is clients who already possess a sense of discipline, such as those who have studied dance for years, or who have run their own companies, building them from ground up, that excel in maintaining their journals. They have already made discipline a part of their everyday lives and understand both the rewards of applying discipline, as well as the consequences of failing to maintain that discipline. Those who fail to attempt to apply it in the first place may have a more difficult time conceptualizing either end of the spectrum. Regarding the act of keeping a journal as a job requirement, however, is one way to begin to apply discipline and work towards the act itself becoming a habit.

## STAYING ON COURSE

Typically, a person who applies discipline to their life is able to stick to a schedule. The head of a company will hold daily or weekly meetings, set aside certain times of the day to take care of particular tasks to make sure their company runs smoothly and that any problem areas are recognized and addressed quickly. A professional dancer will maintain a strict practice and workout schedule, carefully monitoring their activities in order to enhance their abilities and avoid possible injury.

It is easy to see how important discipline and the use of a schedule are to these individuals, but you don't have to be a CEO or a ballerina to understand and relate to this concept. Even parents, whose goal is to have their child do their best in school, has to maintain a highly disciplined schedule. They have to ensure that the child gets enough sleep, has a decent breakfast, understands and completes their schoolwork on time, and devotes an adequate amount of time to reading, while limiting the amount of time the child spends watching television or playing video games.

## COMPILING DATA

Just as kids tend to have certain times of the day set aside to do their homework, you should also set aside time during the day to work on your trading journal. Typically, the sooner you do so, the better. This will help prevent you from putting it off so long that you decide to not even do it that particular day. I have already discussed certain journaling techniques that you can apply throughout the day, keeping track of your ongoing thoughts regarding your positions and the market, the emotions you are experiencing throughout a trade's development, and the reasoning behind your actions.

It is ideal to wait until after the session is over to print out charts of the day's activities. This way, you can view how the remainder of the day played out, particularly in the case of a day trade, and use this information as an integral part of your trade analysis. If you scalp,

> Ideas concerning trade development should always be recorded as close to the actual moment they occur as possible since they can be difficult to recreate in the same perspective after the fact.

you may be able to begin this step intraday by recording the morning's trades during lunch and then addressing afternoon trades following the market close. If you position trade, you can print out charts for the day in which an action such as an entry or exit takes place, and then wait until the weekend to capture the progress.

The sooner you can capture the data the better. If you don't, then it is easy to find yourself trying to catch up all at once on the weekends or even several weeks down the road. By this point, you can become so overwhelmed by the process of data collection that you have neither the time nor the desire to set aside additional time to review the data and reflect upon it in order to draw conclusions about how you are progressing as a trader.

## SEARCHING FOR PATTERNS

Once you have all your data at hand and have recorded your thoughts and actions intraday, as well as the charts and follow-up afterwards, it is imperative to set aside a time to study your journal in order to pick out the patterns in your style. This time is necessary in order to focus in on where both your strengths and weaknesses are, and to help you develop rules that are designed to guide you throughout the trading day.

Even though many of your journal entries may seem incredibly mundane and filled with details that do not change much from one trade or one day to the next, by making it a habit to review and reflect upon your actions, patterns will emerge. You will begin to see, for example, which times of the day yield the greatest results and which cause you the greatest difficulty.

By identifying patterns in terms of the time of day, you can develop strategies for controlling your actions at these times as well. A good example would be if you discovered that only certain types of setups work well for you over the noon hour. You can then use this knowledge to eliminate other setups and focus on maximizing your gains on the ones to which you are already most suited. Alternately, you may find that under certain conditions you almost always lose, so you can then make a conscious choice to stay out of the market when you see those conditions developing. If you are not sure if your observations are accurate long term, you can at least minimize your position size while you test out your theory.

## REVIEW AND REFLECTION

I prefer to do most of my review and reflection on the weekend. It is during this time that I will categorize my positions for the week and compare them to similar setups I have traded in the past. This works well because it takes me "away from the front line" as they say, and puts me in "the strategy room." I am not focused on all the action still developing in the market and getting wrapped up in "the next thing." Instead, I am able to maintain a clearer view of the larger picture. If I find that I have had a particularly difficult day, I will often pull back and retreat for the remainder of the week until I have had the time to compare my most recent actions to those of the past to determine where things are most likely going wrong. If you cannot identify an issue and work out an objective solution to try to correct the problem, then you may likely find yourself simply digging a deeper hole.

Compiling your trading data and the emotional aspects that go along with it is the first part of the schedule you must maintain. Secondly, you must fit in time for reflection and analysis of that data. A third segment of time should be devoted to reviewing the lessons you have learned and the strategies you have developed. I keep a "cheat sheet" of my most common mistakes, as well as my favorite patterns in the front of my loose-leaf journal. I update this rather frequently just to keep it fresh, and I read through it at the beginning of every day.

Ideally, this is something that should be done several times throughout the day since it is easy to become distracted and lose focus. Some traders will find this review necessary to repeat more often than others, and some may struggle with it even when they feel they have resolved to take this step.

## TRICKS & TECHNIQUES — AN EXAMPLE

One client that I worked with found that he was making the same mistakes in almost every position he encountered, but he could not seem to break the bad habits he had developed. Even though he read over his notes on techniques to deal with the issue, when the trading day was underway, he became so wrapped up in the action that he lost track of his rules. In order to break this habit and put him on the correct path, we needed some way to break up his negative concentration intraday to help him refocus.

In order to combat my client's negative focus, I had him bring an alarm clock into his office. I then had him place it on the opposite side of the room so that he would have to physically get up and cross the room to turn it off. It was set it to go off every 30 minutes in between market correction periods, which would be when he was most likely in a position.

> Market correction periods are times of the day where the market is most likely to reverse or break out of a range; for that reason, they are times of the day when many positions are initiated.

When the alarm clock went off I had my client read through his rules list and make sure that if he was in a position at that time, that he was applying the rules he had written down. We had to shake things up a bit using different sounds, adjusting the times based upon when he was the most active, etc., to keep him on his toes, but he soon began to adjust his habits in favor of those that worked *for* him as opposed to *against* him. Whenever he starts to get off track, he will bring in that alarm clock again.

# EXCUSES, EXCUSES

Keeping a journal and maintaining the steps necessary for it to be successful, like any resolution, will not quickly translate into a habit for many people. A now-famous quote by a Mr. J. R. Todd begins with: "The wayside of business is full of brilliant men who start out with a spurt and lacked the stamina to finish." Although we may be diligent to begin with, it is very easy for us to begin to come up with excuses for putting it off. "I'll do it later," or "I know I did the same thing on this trade as the last one, so I don't need to record this one," or "I took so many trades today that I will just write about a couple of them," are all common reasons to delay making an entry.

> Some of my own common excuses include: "My kids just got home, so I'll do it after supper," or "I was up all night working on this book, so I'll just catch up on the weekend."

Although you may think that these seem like legitimate explanations for delaying updates to your journal, what happens when supper is finished and the kids then need help with their homework, or the weekend comes around and the distraction of having others around or plans for outings with friends and family eat away time? If you are like me, you will find that more often than not, if you put something off until you "have more time," it may not get accomplished at all. So, ask yourself, "Would I have taken the time to do it if my job had depended upon it?" In other words, if you were working a "normal" 9-to-5 job, and you would be fired or at least have your pay severely docked because you did not complete your journal, would you still have neglected it?

Now, consider for a moment—by failing to apply discipline, you will not be able to easily recognize where your true faults are. Nor will you be able to sit down and consider what acts are necessary to overcome them. To use my previous analogy: You may have failed to notice that there were a couple of white spots on one of the leaves of your tomato plant or overlooked the seriousness of what those spots signified. And like me, before you knew it, your plant was beyond saving, or at the point where the effort to save it was so daunting that you gave up. If the tomato plant was your trading account, wouldn't it make sense to identify the problem right away and search out a solution?

Additionally, if you fail to take the actions needed to make the act of keeping a journal and reflecting upon it a habit, you won't make the same progress towards understanding and cultivating your strengths as a trader that you could have had you maintained discipline. When you stumble upon a pattern or type of market that favors your personality, you may not be able to recognize it for what it is, or be able to push yourself to take full advantage of it. Alternately, you may fail to recognize the signs that point to a repetition of this same positive market environment in the future.

## THE COSTS ARE TOO HIGH
## TO NEGLECT YOUR JOURNAL

When put in this light, isn't it obvious that by neglecting your journal, you are in fact costing yourself money? You have either cost yourself money by failing to mend or overcome your faults, or you have cost yourself money by failing to see the opportunities at your doorstep. Either way, you have docked your own pay and may also be at risk of being fired, if you have let your bad habits persist for too long, or do not make enough progress to foresee yourself easily attaining your goals or reaching a point at which your efforts feel justified. The consequences of failing to maintain discipline in this area of your life are now more substantial than merely having to run up to the store if you run out of tomatoes.

# BUT MOM, I DON'T WANT A JOB!

I know you are agreeing with me up to this point, right? "Yes, you are absolutely, 100%, completely and totally correct, Toni! That makes perfect sense!" is what is probably going through your head about now…or at least it should be! The transformation itself, however, from a realization into an act can be difficult. Most traders, in fact, know that they should be keeping a trading journal, yet many fail to do so. Some may have begun to keep a journal at some point, but could not figure out how to use it in a manner that was beneficial to their progress, and so they gave up. Others may have started, but did not take the time to gather enough information for it to be useful. Some may have also done so to an extent, knowing that the end result would be helpful, but still failed to maintain it. Most, however, have chosen not to keep one at all.

You can no longer claim to not know *how* to keep a journal, and you obviously can see how keeping one would be beneficial, or else you wouldn't have made it this far in this book. So, keeping this in mind, let's look at what is going on in terms of *choice* and why you may not be keeping a journal already, or why you began one in the past, but failed to maintain it, or are struggling to maintain one currently.

Although keeping a journal can be viewed as rather tedious and not a job we are excited to dive into every day, do not be discouraged! Some people take to it naturally and enjoy the challenges of uncovering new secrets about themselves and their trading styles. Others view it as a chore and something they dread at the end of every day. If you find that you tend to fall into the latter of the two categories, don't worry! Even though journaling may never become a passion, you can still change your mindset to the point that you feel positive about accomplishing this task. To prove my point, let me share with you a conversation I had with two accomplished young individuals who can easily be divided between the two mindsets listed above.

The individuals to whom I am referring are my children. While in the process of writing this book, I had a discussion with my children about jobs and what they want to be when they grow up. My daughter was nine, going on ten, and she lamented for years that she was not yet old enough to have a job. She couldn't wait to join the workforce and earn her own money. While her ultimate goal was to become a trader, she said that she would like to trade and invest part-time, while having another career as well. My son, on the other hand, had just turned six and vehemently proclaimed that he would "NEVER have a job!" He didn't want one and never would, according to his own words. While my daughter enjoyed seeking out new subject matter and writing about her experiences, it was often a matter of "pulling teeth" to get my son to sit still long enough to read two pages, let alone stick to any task requiring a greater level of perseverance. (Luckily, this is no longer the case!)

While the motivations behind my son's proclamation may never be positively known, it occurred to me that it would be necessary to change his way of thinking about what it meant to "have a job," and to turn it from a negative into a positive.

Although my daughter pointed out that if he did not have a job, he would have to sleep on the streets and would not be able to buy anything to eat, my son was not at all deterred by this information and remained resolute.

I was quiet for a few minutes as I wondered just how to approach what was obviously a topic that my son felt very strongly about. I quickly realized that while my son may feel strongly against the concept of holding a job, he absolutely loved going to school. He was constantly relating stories to me about all the fun things he did in school and what he learned and how he couldn't wait to go back the next day.

So I pointed out, "But, you already have a job."

"I do not!" he replied emphatically.

"Of course you do," I stated. "You go to school. This is your job. Every day I get up. I go to my office. I work on my computer. Every day, you get up, you go to the bus stop, and you go to school. While you are there you work on things. You practice your reading and writing and you learn new things. So, school is your job."

"Mom, school is not a job! School is fun!" he proclaimed.

I then pointed out that I think my job is fun also. I read on the computer. I write about the market. I learn new things. I talk to my friends, etc. All of which he is doing as well, minus the market aspect! Although not yet ready to admit that I may actually have a point, his demeanor began to shift. The next morning, the kids came in to say good-bye before they headed out to the bus stop. They always head out the door saying, "Have a good day at work!" This time, however, I beat them to it. I said, "I love you! Have a good day at work!" My boy grinned and responded with an exasperated, "Mooom!" then he paused and added, "Okay!" When he came home that afternoon, I asked him how his day "at work" went and he replied, "I had a GREAT day!" and proceeded to pull out a green cutout bear his teacher gives to kids that did well on that particular day. On the front it read, "GREAT JOB!" It quickly became a running joke at our house that when the kids head to school we would wish each other a "great day at work!"

## CHANGING YOUR MINDSET

By taking a concept that my son felt very negatively about and comparing it to another activity towards which he had already developed a positive attitude, I was able to help him shift his negative mindset regarding what it meant to have a job to a positive one. Okay, granted, changing the mindset of a six-year-old may seem like a rather easy feat to accomplish, unless, of course, you've actually met a six-year-old and attempted to do so! Six-year-olds are not well-known for their strong reasoning skills. More often than not, when asked to explain an action or a feeling, the response will include something along the lines of a simple "because," or a bewildered "I don't know." These were the responses my son had given when I initially asked him why he didn't want to have a job, although they are typical responses to other topics of discussion as well. If you attempt to press for a more detailed answer, the child will often become confused or respond with whatever they think you might want to hear.

Interestingly, in the past when I have asked many of my clients why they do not keep a trading journal, they tend to give me the same type of reply! They may simply "not know" why they feel the way the do. You may be wondering why I am comparing the points of view of a child to those of an adult, but think about it. How we approach life as adults is not necessarily more complex than how we approached it as children. In order to make something unpleasant become bearable or even enjoyable, we must convince ourselves of its worth. Knowing or understanding that something is worthwhile does not ensure that we will be content in undertaking a particular task or that we can easily overcome our negative mindset. The first step in the process of doing so is to understand why we express negativity towards something to begin with.

# WORK, THEN PLAY

Let's take a look at the conversation with my son and his declaration about his future job prospects, or lack thereof! The most likely explanation for my son reacting negatively to the concept of having a job is that he equated the terms "job" and "work" with other tasks he did not like to complete because of the additional effort involved. One such example would be putting away his clothes "nicely," as opposed to the more rapid and hence, preferred method of wadding them up and shoving them in his drawer. He would much rather be playing than "working." Taking the additional time to fold and hang up his clothes detracted from the time that could be spent working on building his Lego version of Busch Gardens.

My son's feeling that he "had better things to do" than put his clothes away nicely is not very different from the excuses many adults have for failing to maintain discipline in their lives, whether they are conscious of it or not. Essentially, they would much rather be playing! It is much easier to gravitate towards activities that require very little active mental participation than to actively engage your brain in an endeavor. When considered in this light, my son's play time is actually more likely to be a positive activity and a better reason for his wishing to hurry through other tasks than the excuses adults are likely to gravitate towards. At least the creation of his Lego amusement park, complete with dinosaur patrons, involves the extensive use of his imagination. Flipping through videos online or watching the newest television sitcoms are not quite the same thing! And yet, it is rather amazing the amount of time a person can waste on these activities while still claiming to not have enough time for more rewarding ventures.

An enlightening exercise for anyone to carry out, regardless of how you currently think you spend your time, is to take one week and keep a diary of how you spend your time throughout that week. Be honest with yourself and try to act as you normally would, without implementing any changes in your lifestyle. Also, when you begin a task, consider how much time is spent on the actual task as opposed to distractions that have grabbed your attention and delayed the completion of the task you have undertaken. For instance, if you sit down to pay your bills online, how much of your time is spent taking care of your finances as compared to watching the television across the room or chatting with a friend online?

At the end of the week, figure out about how much time would be needed to complete tasks that you feel would be beneficial for your life and your future, such as the amount of time it would take to maintain your trading journal. Since your health is also extremely important to your long-term success, throw in a few hours a week for exercise as well, if this is not already part of your routine. Now examine the activities in your life that did virtually nothing to improve your quality of life, and compare that to the amount of time necessary to implement the activities that would improve it. You will likely find that even after you have figured in time for your trading journal *and* an exercise program, you still have a lot of time left over to "relax."

# THE POWER OF THOUGHT

Another barrier that you may have to overcome in your quest to make a trading journal a part of your work ethic is the collective mindset in which disliking ones' job is "a universally recognized truth." We are told on a daily basis by the media, by our friends, and by our families that jobs make us miserable. There are constant representations of the cranky and consistently unsatisfied boss, the obnoxious co-worker, the over-demanding client, and so on everywhere we turn. Just change the channel on the television to an episode of *The King of Queens* or *Roseanne*, attend a family reunion, or invite your closest friends over for a barbeque, and the chances are high that it will not be long before you experience this mindset first hand.

Children are also exposed to this mindset on a regular basis, if not from their own family, then from friends, or on television where other kids are constantly complaining about things they are expected to do, even to the extent that they are whining or throwing some sort of temper tantrum. Children who see such behavior on a regular basis then assume that this is the norm and an expected response to things they are asked to do, but may not desire to do.

If you can easily relate to the idea that a job is something to complain about, then the concept of a trading journal as a job requirement may not be something you can easily embrace. While you recognize that discipline is necessary in order to succeed, you may still find yourself resistant to making a real commitment and fail to develop the habit of journaling. Somehow you are going to have to push past this resistance and break free from this negative mindset.

Start by asking yourself why you resist in the first place. Just as my son responded, you may also be saying to yourself in a bewildered tone, "I don't know!" If you find that you are constantly starting and stopping at this task, or failing to find yourself motivated to act in the first place, it can very easily lead to frustration. One goal of a journal is to help you deal with frustrating issues that have arisen in your trading, leading to questions such as "Why do I always...?" or "Why can't I just...?" By studying your actions, you can step back and take an objective approach to finding solutions to these issues. If you find yourself asking these same questions when it comes to keeping a journal in the first place, then this frustration is magnified.

## CONFIDENCE IS KEY

Your success in the market, or any area of your life, is often tied more directly to your belief in your ability to succeed than by any other factor. Regardless of how well you plan and how hard you work, if you don't believe that you can succeed, then it's likely that you never will. Negative attitudes are strongly tied to failure. In trading, these negative attitudes will lead you to hesitate on great setups, take higher-risk setups because they have given you more time to consider them, bail on positive positions simply because you have a gain and are afraid of a loss, fail to hold your stops, or any other number of problems that are tied more to your emotions than to reason. It is actions such as these that generate questions such as, "Why do I always…?" In order to succeed, you have to re-solve to defeat this negative mindset.

# TONI'S TIPS

## Chapter 11

- Take the act of maintaining a trading journal seriously. If you wish to turn a desire to trade into a lasting career—even just a part-time one—you have to develop a firm habit of stick-to-it-tiveness by turning your desire to succeed into a full resolve to succeed. Consider the act of keeping a journal to be a job requirement. This is one way to begin to apply discipline and work towards that act itself becoming a habit, as opposed to a chore.

- Set aside time during the day to work on your trading journal. Typically, the sooner you do so, the better. This will help prevent you from putting it off so long that you decide to not even do it that particular day. Ideas concerning trade development should always be done as close to the actual moment they occur as possible since they can be difficult to recreate in the same perspective after the fact.

- Compiling your trading data and the emotional aspects that go along with it will not get you very far if you don't fit in the time for reflection and analysis of that data. This is something that is easier to do in larger blocks of time, like on the weekend, when you can sit down and pore over the week's activity and compare it to how you have traded in the past.

- Create a "cheat sheet" of your most common mistakes, as well as your favorite patterns. Review them at the beginning of each trading day, perhaps even several times throughout the day, to help keep on track and keep emotional decisions at bay.

- When faced with a string of losses, step back and take a break. Update your journal to include these most recent trades and study how they compare to other trades you took using similar strategies. What distinguished them from past winners? Did you stick to the rules you established for those particular strategies? Taking the time to reflect can allow you to cool your emotional responses, regroup, and return to trading with renewed confidence and resolve. Don't avoid taking the time to do this, since failure to do so will generally result in digging an even larger hole and making even more decisions based upon emotional responses versus logical ones.

- Take time to step back and think about what the tangible benefits of maintaining a trading journal will be on your quality of life. Ask yourself the following questions: What impact will these benefits have on your lifestyle and that of your family or future family? How much do you truly desire these benefits? What are other things you do throughout the day that contribute very little to your life? How much time do they take out of your day? How much of this time are you willing to trade for the pursuit of something that will allow you to achieve your longer-term goals? Is it really worth sacrificing these goals in favor of spending an extra hour staring at a television screen or playing a video game? Really think about it...

## A STEP FURTHER

By the time you have reached this chapter, you already know the benefits of maintaining a trading journal and how it can dramatically improve your results, but many traders will still fail to do so. Maintaining discipline and following through with the journaling process requires discipline. Think back to other goals you have had throughout your life. Now, write down the answers to the following questions:

What are some of the goals you set for yourself and yet still failed at, and what are some you accomplished?

_____

_____

_____

_____

_____

_____

_____

_____

What steps did you take to reach your goals when you were successful, and where did you fall short when you were not?

_____

_____

_____

_____

_____

_____

What are your goals in trading?

_____

_____

_____

_____

_____

What types of things do you foresee in your life or within your personality that might hold you back and what can you do to push past these roadblocks?

_____

_____

_____

_____

_____

_____

For Toni's answer, go to www.traderslibrary.com/TLEcorner.

# REWARD AND MOTIVATION

## WHAT WILL IT TAKE?

In order to reach the point where a journal can be used to advance your trading skills, you have get to the point at which you are maintaining the journal in the first place. If you find that you are having a great deal of difficulty staying on task; if you feel that you keep butting your head up against a brick wall when trying to implement this form of systematic research and reflection, then you should look at what steps can be implemented into your everyday life to help you push through this wall. What will it take to change your mindset?

I am sure you have heard it said that plants do better when you talk to them and give them positive input. Whether this is true or not, and whether the fact that my tomato plants failed because I neglected to talk to them is still open for debate. What is proven, however, is that people who are rewarded and praised for their genuine efforts tend to go further and persist at a task longer than those who receive little to no encouragement.

You already know that the ultimate reward for maintaining discipline in the markets will be active account growth and a portfolio that you are proud to call your own. You can then use this increase in wealth to realize other dreams and ambitions. These long-term goals may not be tangible enough at present, however, to serve as motivations along the way. The fact that they are long-term can actually be one more thing holding you back. How many people can honestly say they will be satisfied with the prospect of a reward at some indeterminate point in the future versus instant gratification today? Even if the future reward may be great indeed, for many people, it may not be something that they can fully appreciate at this particular point in time. There are many visualization techniques and methods for helping to make these longer-term goals more realistic to you in the present, but that is a topic for another book! In the meantime, let's address what can be done immediately to keep you on the right path.

# THE POWER OF PRAISE

Like most parents, mine wanted me to be happy and do well in life. After starting me on the path to do well in school, however, they simply expected me to continue to do so. I was "the good student," and it was assumed that I would continue to be. This expectation, however, came with very little encouragement. In high school, I had a couple of teachers to whom I owe a great deal of my academic success. They pushed me to think outside the box and challenged me to strive higher. In college, particularly at a large university, it can be much more difficult to make such connections and, therefore, more difficult for someone who is just "a good student" to thrive.

Being rather shy for most of my life, I did not make an effort to seek out positive role models and mentors that would challenge me and provide me with the encouragement I was lacking while away at college. Although I remained on "the expected path" to begin with, taking honors courses as part of a full course load—with no real goal in mind for where my life was heading—I began to slack off in school. I skipped classes, cut my course load and began to put in more hours at a job I did not particularly enjoy. At about this time I got rather lucky. I happened into the markets and once again began to feel challenged. I plunged into this new arena with gusto, and within a relatively short period of time, my work received the notice of a major trading education site that recruited me. Soon I began to work with other traders, helping them reach their goals. As a result, I unwittingly found the praise and encouragement I needed to succeed by sharing my knowledge with others and aiding in their pursuit of success.

## PRAISE AS A MOTIVATING FORCE

Although I realize now what the role of praise played in my current success, the concept of it as a motivating force in a person's life was not one that I fully appreciated until I became a foster parent. Not once did any child I had under my care come to me thinking they could be successful, particularly in school. The phrases I heard most often were "I can't do it," or "I don't know how." Another that was extremely common is "I am stupid." This is a declaration nearly all of them made at some point or another. When children say such things, they are looking for someone to reassure them that what they say is not true. They are seeking praise. As adults, it is easy to get these same phrases in our heads, even unintentionally, whenever we seem to be stuck and not able to make progress at a task. I hear them from time to time, in one form or another, whenever I work with a client who has gotten stuck making the same mistake repeatedly and is trying to break free from this cycle. "Toni, I must be stupid, because even though I know I am wrong, I keep doing it!"

It can be next to impossible to break bad habits if you are so upset over them to begin with that you can't step back and remove yourself from the emotional baggage these habits have created. If you think you are stupid and that something is hopeless, you are not likely to make any positive progress towards reversing that mindset and reaching your goals. Instead of focusing on these thoughts, however, put them aside and focus on the things that you have done well with, and use this positive mindset to develop solutions to tasks that are causing you difficulty. Using discipline to maintain your trading journal is one way to force yourself to do just that.

## IT HAPPENS TO THE BEST OF US

Everyone gets discouraged. Everyone has moments where they think, "How am I ever going to get this right?" and will feel frustrated from the effort. It is at times like this where praise can help motivate you to push past these insecurities. I experienced such a moment while I was working on the manuscript for this very book. I was completely overwhelmed by the constant interruptions of everyday life and began to become quite discouraged. I started to wonder if I was ever going to be free from enough distractions to be able to sit down to get it completed. It did not take long, however, to realize that the act of being frustrated would not get me any closer to my goal. I had to quite deliberately refocus my thoughts away from those negative feelings of frustration and back to positive ones.

As a point of reference, I thought back to when I had when I completed my first CD course and the sense of accomplishment I had felt at that point in time. I also went back and read over some of the emails and letters I'd received that thanked me for the course, as well as for the numerous webinars, lectures, and other events I've done in the past to help other traders. I then projected these feelings forward and focused upon the sense of accomplishment I knew I would feel once this project was also completed. While I know that not everyone who reads this book will apply the lessons I've talked about, many of them, such as yourself, will do so, and benefit greatly as a result. Taking the time to review and reflect upon positive accomplishments in the past was crucial to helping me quickly get back on track.

Your trading journal serves as a record of your own accomplishments. The notes you make in your journal when you have succeeded in making a breakthrough in your trading, or have merely followed your plan perfectly on a given trade, are positive reminders that you can return to, which help to refocus your efforts and show you that you can indeed succeed.

# GO BUY ICE CREAM!

Praising yourself is not an easy feat, and at times, false praise can be more detrimental than no praise at all. Some of the foster children I have cared for were, in fact, accustomed to praise, but they received it for everything, no matter what kind of effort they had actually put into what they were doing. I had a rather monumental run-in with a school one day a few years back regarding one particular child. They had called and explained that the boy had been causing trouble in class and would need to be taken home for the remainder of the day. After a 30-minute conference during which they proceeded to tell me the ways in which he was acting out and all of the difficulty they were having with him, they told me how they pulled him out of class earlier in the day, gave him extra recess, and then sent him to the nurses' offices where they gave him a snack while he waited for me to arrive to take him home. Then, they informed me that the boy was scared he was going to be in trouble, so they told him that I was there because I had something special planned for him and that I should take him to get some ice cream on the way home.

This story, while it may seem rather shocking at first, is not nearly as unusual as you might think. In fact, you probably run into the same thing on a daily basis. Let's take the same idea, and put it into the context of our own actions. If you have had a very rough day in the market and the closing bell has finally rung, what do you do?

Do you sit down and force yourself to review what happened on that day that led up to your failure? Or, do you watch television, have a drink, relax at the pool, or some other activity that you feel will "take away some of your stress"? In other words, do you go treat yourself to ice cream?

In the story of my foster son, it is easy to see how the school was rewarding his negative behavior. If doing something wrong receives constant encouragement, such as extra recess or a snack in the nurses' office, what is the point of changing that behavior? If we have a rough day in the market, and instead of addressing those issues by completing our trading journals and studying and analyzing where we went wrong and how to prevent it in the future, we go watch television or go out to dinner, then we are no better than the school that told me to take my foster son out for ice cream after causing disruptions all day.

Of course, he did not get ice cream. Instead we went home, discussed what had happened during his day and tried to address why it happened. He lost privileges and had to write a letter to his teacher apologizing for his behavior and explaining the things that he would work on in order to prevent a reoccurrence of the same problems. Merely having one day in which he had to really deal with the consequences of his actions did not immediately change his behavior, but by approaching each day and each incident in the same manner, he soon began to progress. This discipline, coupled with honest and deserved praise for his improvement in both his social interactions and school performance began to transform him. He no longer referred to himself as "stupid" and had fewer and fewer problems dealing with his peers.

# CONTINUED DISCIPLINE

Of course, this type of system must be maintained in order to have lasting results. So, let's take it a step further. While I only cared for that particular foster child for about two months, my son has been with me on and off since he was placed with me in foster care at 18 months old. He had just turned six when I began writing this book and had been with me full-time for about two years. Both he and his sister had attitudes towards school that were similar to that of the young boy in the previous story. Nearly every day, however, we sit down, talk about the things that went both right and wrong at school, and work through the things they struggle with, whether it's a subject in school or a problem they are having with a friend. My time, from about 4:00 pm to 8:30 pm every day, is typically theirs.

Although both of my kids are now at the top of their classes, new problems and situations always arise. One day my son came home with an "orange note." This basically meant he had done something that the teacher felt warranted my attention. In this case, he had "poked" another child repeatedly. However good-natured it may have been, it obviously disrupted class. I had a webinar presentation about to begin and didn't have time to sit down and talk with him right away about what had happened. My daughter, in a very chipper voice, said, "Don't worry mom, I will talk with him." When I came in an hour later, my daughter told me how they had had "a good talk" about what had happened and my son proudly handed me a piece of paper with the front side repeating the words, "I will not poke." This was his equivalent of a journal entry. The fact that he could write so well was itself a huge accomplishment! He then explained to me why he shouldn't do things like that in school and what he should do if someone poked him, as opposed to poking them back. I had to work very hard not to laugh. Not only was his demeanor amusing because he was very proud of his work to improve himself, but I was incredibly proud that they had both taken to heart the lessons I had taught them and that they were now applying them without any input at all from me or anyone else!

The types of discussions my kids are now accustomed to are very similar to what goes into a trading journal. By talking through both the positive things and praising them for their progress, as well as discussing the negative things and making sure they understand that it is not acceptable and that they will not be rewarded for such behavior, they have steadily and consistently made progress in not only how they deal with school, but also how they interact with the world in general.

This did not happen overnight however, and there are always setbacks. Most kids, like most adults, are going to be hesitant to talk about their feelings, let alone sit down and write out what can be done to alter them. As I witnessed however, over time, this system of self-reflection, when carried out consistently, becomes a habit and is no longer even something to be dreaded, but rather expected, and viewed in a positive light.

My son woke up the morning after receiving his "orange note," eagerly anticipating his return to school, where he would have the chance redeem himself and to earn a "green bear" for having a "good day at work." He had been reminded of this reward and how great it felt to receive it when he talked with his sister. He must have remained determined to obtain that reward and the praise he knew would come with it, because that very afternoon, he walked in the door and enthusiastically presented me with not only his green bear, but also a note from the teacher telling me about his excellent day at school.

# REWARD YOURSELF!

My daughter served as the journal of sorts for my son when she reminded him of what actions were necessary to reach his goal of a green bear. By using your journal to focus on the positive aspects of your trading, you can create a reward system that will encourage you to maximize your strengths. For example, if you find one strategy that works well for you, then reward yourself when you take a position using that setup and follow your guidelines for the setup successfully. Go buy yourself that ice cream! Adjust this reward system as you develop as a trader, so that it is always something that you must make an effort to achieve. This creates that system of instant gratification that can help keep you on the right path while you work towards a more substantial, longer-term goal.

The concept of reward and praise can also be used in maintaining your journal in the first place. Set aside times of the day to complete your journal entries and to reflect upon them. If you maintain your journal for an entire week, completing it at the time you have scheduled, then plan on doing something special on the weekend that you might not otherwise do, such as going out for dinner. By initiating such a system, you are not only being rewarded for the progress you are making in your trading, but more importantly, for taking the steps necessary to make that progress in the first place.

## REWARD FOR A REASON

Earlier I talked about how we often reward ourselves as merely a way to "get away" and relax after a stressful day. This is a habit you have to break, or at least mitigate. If you go out to dinner on a regular basis, or go directly to the living room and turn on the television every day after the market closes, then you are taking away the value these activities can have. My kids are already quite aware that things such as watching television and going swimming are privileges and not rights. They are things they get to do when all their other work is completed; they are rewards that are withheld if they stray off course. When we go out to a movie, a museum, or spend a day at the beach, these are rewards that do not occur as often, and so they are more meaningful.

Reward yourself for your discipline and for your success, not for the sake of reward itself. If you take this same approach in your own life and develop a similar mindset when it comes to your trading, then you will soon find that you are accomplishing things you had never before visualized as possible. Before you know it, your actions will have become habit. Hopefully you will not cheat very often, and you will find that when you cannot reward yourself because you have neglected to follow your plan, it will deepen your resolve to succeed and follow through with your intentions for the next day or next week in order to obtain that reward.

# DON'T BE AFRAID OF MISTAKES

If you do fail to meet a short-term goal, such as completing your journal on a given day, do not be discouraged! It is typical to fall off track every now and then. Success as a trader does not happen all at once. A seed, once planted, does not immediately transform into a hearty, mature plant. It takes time for things to grow, and your abilities as they relate to the market are no different. It takes time to develop the skills, as well as the discipline, to reach a level whereby you too can view yourself as a professional in this field.

# A WAY OF LIFE

Notice that when an individual resolves to lose weight these days, and that resolve is viewed as a serious undertaking, that they no longer use the term "diet." Instead, the concept of a diet is transformed from a temporary regime to a way of life. The choices such individuals make on a daily basis in terms of what they eat, as well as their level of physical activity, will eventually require very little effort to maintain…once they make them a habit.

I have already shown you why keeping a trading journal is important and how beneficial it will be in moving you forward in your trading career. I have also shown you how to keep a journal, how to use the data that you collect to better your understanding of your own strengths and weaknesses, and to develop a system that will allow you to excel. With this knowledge, it is now up to you to take that final step. Make the act of keeping a trading journal a habit.

Keep in mind the words of J.R. Todd, whose quote we examined in Chapter 11: "The wayside of business is full of brilliant men who start out with a spurt and lacked the stamina to finish." He continues by pointing out that, "Their places were taken by patient and un-showy plodders who never knew when to quit." The lesson here is to take it one day at a time and begin each day with a fresh start. Do not worry about getting ahead in great leaps and bounds, but by building upon a series of smaller, yet consistent victories. Most important, do whatever it takes to remain motivated and committed to making your journal as integral a part of your trading as the execution of the entries and exits are. To put it bluntly: Make your resolution resolute!

## TONI'S TIPS

### Chapter 12

- Focus on the things that you have done well with in your life and how they made you feel. Use this positive mindset to develop solutions to tasks that are causing you difficulty. Think about the sense of accomplishment you will feel when you start to see the results of your discipline.

- It can be very hard at times to not "reward ourselves for bad behavior." Don't do it! If you had a difficult day in the markets, address that fact head on. Sit down and think about what went wrong and how to limit such days in the future—even if the situation was exacerbated by outside forces, such as power failure or trouble with your trading platform. This act alone can help you calm down if your emotions are on overdrive. Do not go away fuming or agonizing over your mistakes, or trying to forget about them altogether by sitting down in front of the television or going out for dinner and drinks. In essence, do not reward your bad behavior—even if that behavior was unintentional!

- Don't forget to reward yourself when you DO deserve it! Use your journal to focus on the positive aspects of your trading, and create a reward system that will encourage you to maximize your strengths. For example, if you find one strategy that works well for you, then reward yourself when you take a position using that setup and follow your guidelines for the setup successfully. Go buy yourself an ice cream! Adjust this reward system as you develop as a trader, so that it is always something that you must make an effort to achieve. Additionally, reward yourself for creating positive habits. If you maintain your journal for an entire week, completing it at the time you have scheduled, then plan on doing something special on the weekend that you might not otherwise do. By initiating such a system, you are not only being rewarded for the progress you are making in your trading, but more importantly, for taking the steps necessary to make that progress in the first place.

**A STEP FURTHER**

It's no surprise that human beings perform better when a reward is within their reach and they truly perceive it as attainable. All traders have some motivation for trading. Often their goals are large ones that will take time to achieve. For example, it can take several years before a full-time trader develops consistency and begins to build an account capable of providing a full-time living. In the meantime, it's still extremely important to stay motivated, working towards smaller goals that will lead you to your desired outcome.

Create a list of goals you can work toward in shorter time frames. For example, what can you accomplish within the next several weeks?

_____

_____

_____

_____

_____

What steps do you need to take to reach these goals?

_____

_____

_____

_____

_____

_____

_____

For Toni's answer, go to www.traderslibrary.com/TLEcorner.

# GLOSSARY

**automated trading system (aka autotrading)** – A trading strategy where buy and sell orders are placed automatically based on an underlying system or program. The buy or sell orders are sent out to be executed in the market when a certain set of criteria is met. (Investopedia.com)

**blog** – An online diary; a personal chronological log of thoughts published on a web page; also called weblog or web log. (Dictionary.com) The author of a blog is called a blogger.

**coach** – A person whose help you enlist to reach a certain goal. They generally charge for the time they spend assisting you and will typically tailor activities, lessons, etc. towards helping you reach your goals. (ToniHansen.com)

**correction periods** – The times of the day or times of the year where an individual security or the overall market is most likely to correct from a previous trend move or begin a new one. 2:00 am EST, 13:00 EST, and 14:00 EST are three examples of popular correction periods. (ToniHansen.com)

**day trader** – A trader who holds positions for a very short time (from minutes to hours) and makes numerous trades each day. Most trades are entered and closed out within the same day. (Investopedia.com)

**exchange-traded fund (ETF)** – A security that tracks an index, a commodity, or a basket of assets like an index fund, but trades like a stock on an exchange. ETFs experience price changes throughout the day as they are bought and sold. By owning an ETF, you get the diversification of an index fund as well as the ability to sell short, buy on margin, and purchase as little as one share. Another advantage is that the expense ratios for most ETFs are lower than those of the average mutual fund. When buying and selling ETFs, you have to pay the same commission to your broker that you would pay on any regular order. One of the most widely known ETFs is called the Spider (SPDR), which tracks the S&P 500 index and trades under the symbol SPY. (Investopedia.com)

**forex market (aka FX or foreign exchange market)** – The market in which participants are able to buy, sell, exchange, and speculate on currencies. The currency market is considered to be the largest financial market in the world, processing trillions of dollars worth of transactions each day. The foreign exchange market isn't dominated by a single market exchange, but involves a global network of computers and brokers from around the world. (Investopedia.com)

**fundamental analysis** – A method of evaluating a security which attempts to measure its intrinsic value by examining related economic, financial, and other qualitative and quantitative factors. Fundamental analysts attempt to study everything that can affect the security's value, including macroeconomic factors (like the overall economy and industry conditions) and company-specific factors (like financial condition and management). (Investopedia.com)

**index futures** – A futures contract on a stock or financial index. For each index, there may be a different multiple for determining the price of the futures contract. The S&P 500 Index is one of the most widely traded index futures contracts in the U.S. (Investopedia.com)

**mentor** – A trusted friend, colleague, teacher, or advisor who has greater experience than yourself within a given profession or field of study whom you can turn to for wisdom or advice. (ToniHansen.com)

**moving average** – An indicator frequently used in technical analysis showing the average value of a security's price over a set period. Moving averages are generally used to measure momentum and define areas of possible support and resistance. Moving averages are used to emphasize the direction of a trend and to smooth out price and volume fluctuations, or "noise," that can confuse interpretation. (Investopedia.com)

**one-cancels-all order (OCA) or one-cancels-the-other order (OCO)** – An order stipulating that if one part of the order is executed, then the other part is automatically canceled.

**option** – A financial derivative that represents a contract sold by one party (option writer) to another party (option holder).

The contract offers the buyer the right, but not the obligation, to buy (call) or sell (put) a security or other financial asset at an agreed-upon price (the strike price) during a certain period of time or on a specific date (excercise date). Options are extremely versatile securities that can be used in many different ways. Traders use options to speculate, which is a relatively risky practice, while hedgers use options to reduce the risk of holding an asset. (Investopedia.com)

**Pattern Day Trader (PDT)** – An SEC designation for traders who trade the same security four or more times per day (buys and sells) over a five-day period, and for whom same-day trades make up at least 6% of their activity for that period. An individual deemed a pattern day trader must hold a minimum of US$25,000 in equity in his or her account before being allowed to day trade. This $25,000 equity amount must be maintained in the account at all times because it addresses the additional risks inherent in leveraged day trading activities and ensures that customers, before continuing to day trade, cover any losses incurred in their accounts from the previous day. (Investopedia.com)

**scalper** – A person trading in the equities or options and futures market who holds a position for a very short period of time, attempting to make money off of the bid-ask spread. (Investopedia.com)

**support and resistance levels** – Price zones in a security that serve as barriers when a trend move is underway that can stall or reverse the trend or cause a new trend to begin. When these price zones are underneath the current price of a security, they are called support. When they are overhead, they are called resistance. (ToniHansen.com)

**swing trading** – A style of trading that attempts to capture gains in a stock within one to four days. Swing traders use technical analysis to look for stocks with short-term price momentum. (Investopedia.com) The term can also apply to traders in other securities holding positions aimed at capturing a momentum move on a daily time frame.

**pace (aka momentum)** – How quickly or slowly prices are changing in a security in a given period of time as compared to how quickly or slowly prices changed in the same amount of time in the past. (ToniHansen.com)

**permalink** – a URL that points to a specific blog entry after it has passed from the front page to the archives. A permalink remains unchanged indefinitely. (Reference.com)

**position trader** – A type of stock trader who holds a position for the long term (from months to years). Long-term traders are not concerned with short-term fluctuations because they believe that their long-term investment horizons will smooth these out. (Investopedia.com)

**stop loss** – A stop is designed to limit losses. It is the maximum adverse move you are willing to risk before closing a losing position. A stop loss should ideally be placed under support on a long position and over resistance on a short. (ToniHansen.com)

**tag** – A keyword or term assigned to a piece of information, such as a major or minor topic within a blog entry, that allows a person to quickly locate related entries in a particular blog or forum by entering the tag into a search feature on the site. (ToniHansen.com)

**technical analysis** – A method of evaluating securities by analyzing statistics generated by market activity, such as past prices and volume. Technical analysts do not attempt to measure a security's intrinsic value, but instead use charts and other tools to identify patterns that can suggest future activity. (Investopedia.com)

**tick charts** – This is a type of chart where every trade, or a set number of trades that take place within a security are plotted on a chart. A 100-tick chart, for example, would include data points for every 100 trades that take place within a security, regardless of the size of the position being represented in the trade or the amount of time it takes to establish 100 trades. (ToniHansen.com)

**trading journal** – A record of trading activities, experiences, and reflections, that is kept on a regular basis and is an integral part of the process of developing a sustainable trading system. (ToniHansen.com)

**universal trading account** – A type of trading account that allows you to trade multiple types of securities from within a single account. This type of account can include all or several of the following: stocks, options, forex, bonds, foreign stocks, mutual funds. (ToniHansen.com)

**volume** – The number of shares or contracts traded in a security or an entire market during a given period of time. (Investopedia.com)

# ABOUT TONI HANSEN

Toni Hansen is the President and CEO of the Hansen Finance Group, LLC and Trading From Main Street. Toni began her trading career as an equity swing trader in the mid-1990s and has since expanded into many other sectors of the market. Her style of trading and market analysis transcends both time as well as market vehicles.

Toni is one of the most respected technical analysts and traders in the industry, with a high reputation for accuracy in both bull and bear markets. She is a frequent guest lecturer at trade shows and trading expos, and often speaks on behalf of many of the world's top exchanges, including the CME Group and the International Securities Exchange. Toni is also a repeat contributor to the industry's top financial publications, including *SFO Magazine*, *Your Trading Edge* magazine, *Traders' Journal*, and *Active Trader*, and publishes daily market commentary and market education through her website http://www.tonihansen.com.

**M**arketplace Books is the preeminent publisher of trading, investing, and finance educational material. We produce professional books, DVDs, courses, and electronic books (ebooks) that showcase the exceptional talent working in the investment world today. Started in 1993, Marketplace Books grew out of the realization that mainstream publishers were not meeting the demand of the trading and investment community. Capitalizing on the access we had through our distribution partner Traders' Library, Marketplace Books was launched, and today publishes the top authors in the industry—household names like Jack Schwager, Oliver Velez, Larry McMillan, Sheldon Natenberg, Jim Bittman, Martin Pring, and Jeff Cooper are just the beginning. We are actively acquiring some of the brightest new minds in the industry including technician Jeff Greenblatt and programmers Jean Folger and Lee Leibfarth.

From the beginning student to the professional trader, our goal is to continually provide the highest quality resources for those who want an active role in the world of finance. Our products focus on strategic information and cutting edge research to give our readers the best education possible. We are at the forefront of digital publishing and are actively pursuing innovative ways to deliver content. At our annual Traders' Forum event, our readers get the chance to learn and mingle with our top authors in a way unprecedented in the industry. Our titles have been translated in most major world languages and can be shipped all over the globe thanks to our preferred online bookstore, TradersLibrary.com.

## VISIT US TODAY AT:

### WWW.MARKETPLACEBOOKS.COM & WWW.TRADERSLIBRARY.COM